T4-ABN-213

THE BUTTER BOOK

THE BUTTER BOOK

Anna Stockwell

CHRONICLE BOOKS
SAN FRANCISCO

Text copyright © 2026 by Anna Stockwell.
Photographs copyright © 2026 by Kate Jordan.

All rights reserved. No part of this book may be reproduced in any form without written permission from the publisher.

Library of Congress Cataloging-in-Publication Data available.

ISBN 978-1-7972-3827-2

Manufactured in China.

Food styling by Anna Stockwell.
Prop styling by Raina Kattelson.
Design by Lizzie Vaughan.
Typesetting by Kelsey Cox.

10 9 8 7 6 5 4 3 2 1

Chronicle books and gifts are available at special quantity discounts to corporations, professional associations, literacy programs, and other organizations. For details and discount information, please contact our premiums department at corporategifts@chroniclebooks.com or at 1-800-759-0190.

Chronicle Books LLC
680 Second Street
San Francisco, California 94107
www.chroniclebooks.com

BUTTER TO SCALE →

| 1 TBSP | 2 TBSP | 3 TBSP | 4 TBSP | 5 TBSP | 6 TBSP | 7 TBSP | 8 TBSP |

4 TABLESPOONS = ¼ CUP
4 TABLESPOONS = ¼ CUP
8 TBSP = ¼ LB = ½ CUP

THIS UNIT NOT LABELED FOR RETAIL SALE

CONT

Introduction [p. 10]

A Brief History of Butter [p. 13]

How to Make Butter [p. 18]

A World of Butter Accessories [p. 28]

Butter Buying 101 [p. 33]

Butter Sculptures and Other Fun Ways to Serve Butter **p. 59**

TEN FAVORITE RECIPES

1 Pommes Anna (à la Anna) [p. 73]

2 Grown-Up Buttered Pasta [p. 77]

3 Butter Roast Chicken [p. 79]

4 Butter-Basted Scallops with Beurre Blanc [p. 83]

5 Compound Butter Biscuits [p. 87]

Acknowledgments [p. 108]

ENTS

A Dozen and One Things a Bit of Butter Instantly Makes Better	[p. 40]
How to Make Clarified Butter	[p. 43]
How to Make Compound Butter	[p. 48]
How to Make Whipped Butter	[p. 53]

Butter Boards for Easy Entertaining **p. 65**

THAT DEPEND ON BUTTER

6   Butterscotch Pudding [p. 91]

7   Cultured Butter Oat Shortbread [p. 93]

8   Brown Butter Mochi Cupcakes [p. 97]

9   New Classic Chocolate Chip Cookies [p. 99]

10   Birthday Butter Cake [p. 103]

Index [p. 109]

INTRODUCTION

Do you remember holding a buttercup flower under your friend's chin to find out if they liked butter? If the buttercup cast a yellow glow on their chin, it meant that they clearly did. Everyone I tested this on got a positive result, which didn't surprise me at all as a kid, because of course everyone loves butter. Turns out the shiny, reflective petals of the buttercups in your garden will always cast a yellow glow, regardless of your feelings about butter. But I still believe in the universal appeal of butter. I stand with Julia Child, who famously said, "With enough butter, anything is good."

This little book you're holding is my way of celebrating all the ways that butter makes life better, from enriching your hot morning toast to flavor-boosting a simple steak to ensuring your snack spread at the next cocktail hour is a hit (everyone loves a butter board). We'll look at where butter came from and how it fits into our culinary heritage, how to shop for and serve it, and how to make and flavor it yourself at home.

Western cuisine as we know it today wouldn't exist without butter. It is a building block, alchemical catalyst, and flavor multiplier. As a student in French culinary school, butter loomed large in my training. I watched in awe as I learned how to monter au beurre, which literally translates to mount with butter and means to whisk cold butter into a warm sauce or purée to instantly add body, shine, flavor, and richness. I learned that the way you whisk or melt butter into batter can create completely different textures in cakes and cookies. I discovered that a croissant could never exist without its layers of butter, the steam of which evaporates to lift the layers of dough as it bakes.

The recipes in this book merely scratch the surface of preparations that rely on the transformative power of butter and celebrate its singular flavor. But they're some of my personal favorites, and I hope you'll cook and bake them with eyes newly opened to the importance of butter, from its ability to flavor and crisp potatoes to the way it leavens classic biscuits. More than anything, I hope this book helps you love butter as much as I do, buttercup glow or no.

A BRIEF HISTORY OF BUTTER

9000 BCE — Butter is one of the oldest human-made foods. Its history goes back so far it is hard to separate it from the history of cooking itself, and we can't know exactly when or where it was first made since it predates written records. It is believed to come from the Neolithic period, sometime between 9000 and 8000 BCE, likely somewhere in central Asia. Legend goes that butter was discovered accidentally by nomads who were carrying animal skin pouches full of yak's, sheep's, or goat's milk on long journeys. They observed that the butterfat separated from the buttermilk after hours of agitation and fermentation on the backs of their pack animals. This isn't hard to believe—if you've ever taken a jug of heavy cream on a long and winding car ride, you may have made the same discovery.

4000 BCE — We have documented proof of butter from as far back as 4000 BCE, found in traces of butterfat in pottery, while depictions of churning butter and milking cows can be seen in Sumerian temples from as far back as 2500 BCE. The earliest written records of butter come from Roman times, when it was initially used for medicine and skincare, but not eaten. Meanwhile, we know the ancient Egyptians used butter as part of their mummification process.

2500 BCE

Though ancient Mediterranean people preferred olive oil, butter was a big part of the diet of the ancient Celts, who spread it throughout Northern Europe as they migrated to the British Isles and the Breton coast of France, areas that still have a thriving butter culture today. In the warmer climates of India, butter was clarified into ghee to keep it from spoiling and used as a staple in cooking, medicine, and religious rituals. In Ireland (and other boggy countries), wooden buckets of butter were sunk into the naturally cool and acidic bogs for preservation. This method worked so well that "bog butter" that has recently been uncovered dates from as early as 400 BCE.

400 BCE

Though butter is still made from yak's milk in much of central Asia, the most common butter in the world today is made from cow's milk. This shift happened as cattle farming became more widespread across Europe and the British Isles around 7000 BCE. Cows can produce more milk than other ruminants, and thus cow's-milk butter became plentiful and a culinary staple.

Butter is deeply woven into our languages, religions, and history. We "butter up" our bosses and describe anything smooth to be "like butter." Hindus have been making offerings of ghee to Lord Krishna for centuries, and butter is cited as a food of celebration in the Bible, offered by Abraham and Sarah as a feast for visiting angels. Butter was so beloved in Europe in the Middle Ages that it was forbidden on fast days and during Lent as an ultimate sacrifice. The enterprising Catholic church eventually came up with a "butter indulgence" tax, which forgave this sin—it was so popular it single-handedly funded the building of the "Butter Tower" at Rouen Cathedral in Normandy.

1800s Originally, butter making was done at home in small batches by farmwives and milkmaids. With the dawn of the Industrial Revolution in the Western world, new technological innovations all but erased the traditional methods and women's historic place in dairy production, as butter production moved from the farm to the factory. The advent of refrigeration in the mid-1800s was a game changer, speeding up the butter-making process, prolonging the shelf life of butter without the need for salt, and providing the ability to transport butter longer distances in refrigerated train cars. The most groundbreaking advancement came in 1878 with the centrifugal cream separator, which allowed cream and milk to be instantly separated by rapid spinning. This completely changed the flavor of butter: Before, cream was separated from milk by gravity, a slow process during which the milk takes on ambient bacterial cultures and starts to ferment, giving the resulting butter a funky, savory taste. With instant separation, butter could be made from fresh cream, lending it a sweeter taste, and thus sweet cream butter was born. In the late 1800s, pasteurization (the process of heating liquid to kill bacteria) was introduced to the dairy industry, further extending the shelf life and increasing the fresh taste of butter. The next big leap in butter production technology came along in the 1940s with the invention of the butyrator, a large continuously churning machine that could produce more than a ton of butter per hour. Today, computer-operated butyrators can produce over 22,000 pounds of butter an hour.

Around the same time that industrial butter became the norm, margarine came on the scene and began to cause big problems for the butter industry. It all started in 1869 when Napoleon III, facing butter shortages and a potential war with Prussia, offered a prize to anyone who could come up with a cheaper substitute. A French chemist won the prize with oleo-margarine, a spread made from beef fat flavored with milk. It didn't take off in France, but an American dairy company bought the patent and started mass-producing margarine, which was cheaper and more shelf stable than butter. By the late nineteenth century, the margarine versus butter battle in the United States was political and bitter. Through the Great Depression and WWII, margarine (now made with vegetable oil instead of beef fat) became more popular than butter due to rationing and shortages.

1930s–40s

Beginning in the 1950s, the view of butter shifted from something wholesome and appealing to something unhealthy that should be avoided due to studies (which have since been disproven) that linked heart disease to eating saturated fats. The low-fat diet fads of the 1980s didn't help butter bounce back. At the turn of the twentieth century, Americans were consuming 18 pounds of butter annually per capita; by 1997, that had fallen to 4.1 pounds.

1950s

1980s

1990s

16

Today These days, thanks to a renewed interest in traditional culinary crafts and artisanal foods, as well as a better understanding of the importance of healthy fats as part of a well-balanced diet, butter is once again thriving in the mainstream. Recent decades have seen a resurgence of small-batch butter producers, many of whom are throwing technology by the wayside in favor of traditional and slow butter-making processes. Local butter, grass-fed butter, cultured butter, and slow-churned butter are all being celebrated for their unique flavors; the fact that no two kinds of butter are exactly alike is now recognized as being a very good thing.

> **WELCOME TO THE NEW GOLDEN AGE OF BUTTER! IT'S A DELICIOUS TIME TO BE ALIVE.**

HOW TO MAKE BUTTER

With so much perfectly good butter available anywhere you shop, why, you might ask, would you want to make your own butter? It's not cheaper, it's not faster, and it's never going to be as perfectly textured as the stuff from the industrial butter machines. But it is shockingly satisfying and fun to make. And I've never tasted fresher or creamier sweet cream butter than the batches I've made myself. We should all make our own butter at least once, even if it's just to say you know how to do it.

When choosing cream, quality matters. Look for a "heavy cream" instead of a "whipping cream." Make sure there are no stabilizers or additives—the only ingredient should be cream—and, unless you have a raw milk dealer you trust, make sure the cream has been pasteurized.

If you've ever made whipped cream, you're well on your way to making butter. Keep agitating that cream past soft peaks and the fat will start to separate from the buttermilk, which just needs to be strained away while the fat gets kneaded into butter. Centuries ago, farmwives and milkmaids churned their cream into butter by pumping a wooden paddle up and down in a large, tall crock. You can still purchase one of these butter churns today if you want to go full-on homesteader, but it's easy to make a few sticks' worth of butter with equipment you already have in your kitchen. A stand mixer is the easiest tool to use if you have one, but a food processor, handheld mixer, hand-cranked butter churn, or even a jar with a tightly fitting lid will all get you to good butter eventually, with varying degrees of elbow grease.

[**TO MAKE BUTTER**]

1

Start with at least 1½ cups [360 ml] of heavy cream. Anything less is too hard to work with. That'll get you about ½ cup [113 g] of butter, depending on your cream. I usually use 2 cups [475 ml] of cream and end up with around ¾ cup [170 g] of butter.

2

Pour your cream into the bowl of a stand mixer fitted with the whisk attachment, the bowl of a food processor, a clean bowl with a handheld mixer, the jar of a butter churner, or a glass jar that is at least twice the volume as the amount of cream you are using. Beat on medium speed, process, whisk, churn, or shake until the cream begins to thicken, then increase to high speed until the cream holds stiff peaks like whipped cream.

3

Continue agitating the cream at high speed past the point of whipped cream. Watch as it begins to thicken and goes from white to buttery yellow. When it starts to look curdled, it's about to separate into butter. Stop here and scrape down the sides of your bowl. If you're using a stand mixer or a bowl with a handheld mixer, cover your mixer and bowl with a large dishcloth or plastic wrap so you don't splash buttermilk all over your kitchen and yourself. Continue beating until the buttermilk separates and little butter curds start to clump together into larger curds.

4

Line a strainer with cheesecloth and set it over a bowl. Pour in the butter curds and buttermilk and let the buttermilk seep through into the bowl. Transfer the buttermilk to another container to use in place of skim milk. (Don't be confused that it doesn't taste like the buttermilk you're used to buying at the store—traditional buttermilk is the by-product of making cultured butter, which is how it gets that nice tang.)

5

Move your now-empty bowl fitted with the strainer full of butter curds over to the sink and run very cold water over the curds until the bowl is full, then lift the strainer out of the bowl and dump the water. Do this a few more times until the water runs clear. If it's hot in your kitchen, add ice cubes to the last rinse to chill the butter. Then transfer your bowl to a clean work surface and pull the edges of the cheesecloth to gather the butter curds together. Squeeze them into a tight ball to release as much of the liquid from the butter as possible.

6

Knead the butter a bit to get the rest of the liquid out and ensure a nice, smooth texture. It's best, if possible, to avoid touching the butter with your warm hands. The traditional way to do this is with wooden butter paddles, which have grooves to encourage the water to run down. They work great and can be ordered online for around $15 (and you can use them for rolling gnocchi too). But you can also use your (cold!) hands or a large wooden or silicone spatula. Press the butter between the butter paddles (or against your work surface with your hands or spatula) and pat and knead for a couple minutes until the butter is smoother. At this point you can season to taste with salt or go ahead and turn it into compound butter (page 48).

7

Pat or press the butter into your desired shape, then roll it in parchment paper and refrigerate it until ready to use, up to two weeks. I don't advise using homemade butter in baking recipes, because the water content is unpredictable, and it may mess with your bake.

1

4–5

7

A WORLD OF BUTTER ACCESSORIES

a. **Covered Butter Dish**
For storing butter on the counter or in the fridge, these dishes can be made of plastic, metal, or ceramic, and come in many different sizes and shapes, from shell to house to cow.

b. **Butter Keeper** *(a.k.a. French Butter Crock or Butter Bell)*
Fill the bottom with cold water and the bell with softened butter. Invert the bell of butter into the water to create an airtight seal that keeps the butter spreadable and fresh on the counter.

c. **Vintage Butter Molds**
The pre-industrial dairymaid's tool for shaping and embossing blocks of butter. Some are ceramic, some wood. If wood, soak it in cold water before filling it with softened butter to mold.

d. **Wooden Butter Pat Press**
Mold and easily pop out stamped pats of butter with this old-world tool. Soak it in cold water before filling it with softened butter.

e. **Two-Piece 3D Butter Molds**
Make a 3D butter animal, lemon, or shell by filling both sides of this mold with softened butter, squishing it together, and chilling it until firm.

f. **Butter Curler**
This serrated hook forms elegant curls of butter when you scrape it across a stick of butter.

g. **Coquillor** *(a.k.a. Butter Press or French Butter Dish)*
A silver butter dish and curler in one. Fill the tray halfway with butter and press down to extrude a flower of butter curls.

Butter Blade   h. ─────
Got cold butter you want to spread onto bread? The small holes across one side of this knife make spreadable butter spaghetti when you scrape it across a stick of cold butter.

Butter Slicer   i. ─────
For perfectly portioned pats of butter, press this metal wire-strung device down over a stick of cold butter.

Individual Butter Knife *(a.k.a. Butter Spreader)*   j. ─────
In formal cutlery, this is a short, flat knife with a dull, rounded blade and handle for spreading butter at your individual plate.

Table Butter Knife *(a.k.a. Master Table Knife)*   k. ─────
In formal cutlery, this is a short, non-serrated, sharp, and pointed knife used only for serving butter from a communal butter dish to individual plates—it's not for spreading butter with.

Butter Warmer   l. ─────
Made specifically for melting and pouring butter, this tiny stovetop pot is the most common kind of warmer. Another variety, made to keep melted butter warm at the table, has a stand and a candle underneath or a compartment for hot water.

Butter Paddles   m. ─────
The traditional (and best) tool for kneading and shaping butter without touching it with your hot hands. Some paddles have grooves on them to help dispel water from the butter as you knead it. Either way, soak the wood tools in cold water before using to ensure the butter doesn't stick.

BUTTER BUYING 101

If you've ever stood, frozen with indecision, in front of a vast case of butter in a grocery store, I'm here to reassure you that you are not alone. All the choices staring you down from colorful boxes are overwhelming! Do you go with the cheapest option and grab the store brand? Do you read every label and wonder what all those different names mean? Do you buy the same butter your mom always bought without wondering why? Do you wish I'd just tell you what kind of butter to buy already?

There is no one right choice when it comes to buying butter. The most important thing to know is that you should buy different types of butter for different use cases! Within that, I want you to find brands you personally like the taste of from companies whose practices align with your values and prices fit your budget. Sample as many options as you can to find the right ones for you. Honestly, the process of researching and tasting butter for this book completely changed my butter-buying habits (and thus my cooking and eating) for the better.

Salted vs. Unsalted Butter

Salt is a natural preservative, and before the days of refrigeration, butter was always heavily salted to help keep it fresh. We don't have to worry about that today, but salted butter does keep longer (about four months) than unsalted butter (about two months) in the fridge. It's also safer to keep salted butter out on your counter at room temperature if you want to have easily spreadable butter at any moment.

For bread or baked potatoes, salted butter is best, because everything tastes better with salt. It's also good for cooking with, as it helps season your food for you! Finish your green beans with salted butter and you won't need to add salt to them. Melt salted butter to drizzle over your popcorn, and it might be salty enough just like that.

Not all salted butter is salted equally, though, so recipes that require specific salt measurements should always be made with (and are always developed with) unsalted butter. In baking this is especially important.

Sweet Cream Butter

This is butter made from uncultured, fresh cream. Sweet cream is the type of butter you most likely think of when you think of butter—mild and creamy and pale yellowish-white. It is not actually sweetened—it's just naturally sweet like milk is sweet—and is sold in both salted and unsalted versions. It's great for baking and cooking with. Sweet cream butter wasn't possible until after the mechanical cream separator was invented in the late 1800s. Before then, all butter was cultured butter.

Cultured Butter

The tangy, savory taste of cultured butter was the norm before the advent of mechanical cream separation and pasteurization. Milk had to sit out for a day or more before all the cream would rise to the surface to be skimmed off to make butter, and then it could take several more days to collect enough cream for a batch of butter. In the meantime, the raw milk and cream, exposed to natural bacteria cultures in the air, would gradually ripen and ferment. Since the Industrial Revolution, cultured butter has been made by adding a lactic-acid-producing bacteria to pasteurized cream and allowing it to ferment, carefully monitored to exactly the right amount, before churning it into butter. These days, many "cultured" butters are made as sweet cream butter then flavored with lactic acid cultures after churning. Both ways taste good, and it is honestly kind of hard to tell the difference in the end product. You'll know it's been made the traditional way if the label says "vat-cultured."

Organic vs. Grass-Fed vs. Pasture-Raised Butter

Organic butter is made from the milk of cows fed organic diets, meaning they are not exposed to toxic pesticides, hormones, or GMOs. Some organic butter is also grass-fed, some is pasture-raised, and some is neither.

The main difference between grass-fed and pasture-raised butter is the diet of the cows: Pasture-raised animals spend a lot of time grazing in pastures, but their diet is supplemented with other feed. Grass-fed cows eat 100 percent grass, which means they are also, naturally, pasture-raised. Both options are better for cows and better for the environment because grazing cows are happier cows and produce less methane than grain-fed cows.

Most butter brands will state the exact percentage of grass the cows are fed on the label. The higher the percentage of fresh grass (as opposed to dried grains or straw) a cow eats, the more beta-carotene ends up in the cream, which gives the butter a yellow color and a more intensely "buttery" and grassy flavor. Grass-fed butter also contains a higher concentration of beneficial fatty acids, so it is generally considered a slightly healthier option. I adore the taste of grass-fed butter and stock my fridge with it, but if you're used to the milder flavor of sweet cream butter, you may find it's not to your liking. There's only one way to find out!

European-Style Butter
According to US law, butter must be at least 80 percent fat. European law dictates butter must be at least 82 percent fat. But butter doesn't need to be made in Europe to contain a higher fat percentage—the "European-style" label on American butters like Plugrà refers to the higher fat content.

Two percent may not sound like a big difference, but taste them side by side, and bake with them side by side, and you'll see. More fat equals more flavor and yields cakes and cookies that are more tender, frostings and sauces that are richer and creamier, and a smoother and more luxurious smear on your slice of bread.

European butter is also often cultured, even though it may not advertise the fact on the label. Check the ingredients list to find out—if "live cultures" or "lactic acid" are listed, that means it's cultured and will have that pleasant slight tang.

Irish Butter
In Ireland, they don't culture their butter, but they usually do salt it, though you can find some unsalted Irish butters for sale these days. Irish butter, like European-style, must be at least 82 percent butterfat.

Traditionally, Irish butter is made from cows that graze primarily on grass. The country's moist climate creates lots of fertile green grass, which means those cows are absorbing a lot of beta-carotene, producing an even richer and yellower butter than anywhere else.

Alternative and Nondairy Butter
These days, the butter aisle at the grocery store is filled with almost as many butter substitutes as traditional butter options. You'll see tubs of oil-based "buttery spread" and sticks of vegan butter. Since the FDA banned artificially created partially hydrogenated oils, margarine isn't as bad for you as it used to be, and it can be an acceptable substitute for butter if you need to avoid dairy for health or ethical reasons. Just make sure the buttery spread isn't flavored with milk before you buy it—many of them are! The label should clearly state "dairy-free" to be safe for you. For baking, a buttery spread won't work— look instead for a firm butter substitute sold in

sticks. Miyoko's makes a delicious European-style plant-based butter that works great as a vegan substitute for traditional butter.

In some grocery stores, you can also buy butters made from dairy other than cow's milk. Goat's-milk butter is, like goat cheese, a little tangier and funkier than cow's-milk butter but has a similar texture. Water buffalo butter, similar in taste to Italian buffalo mozzarella, is a fun treat to spread on bread.

Ghee

First things first: Ghee is clarified butter (page 43), but not all clarified butter is ghee. Both are made by heating and skimming butter to remove the milk solids and water, which means many people with dairy sensitivities can safely enjoy them. (These days, machinery exists that allows ghee to be manufactured straight from cream.) No milk solids also means clarified butter has a higher smoke point than butter, so it's better for cooking at high temperatures. Clarified butter is shelf stable and keeps for a very long time. Unlike standard clarified butter, ghee is cooked at low heat for a long time until the milk solids begin to brown, which gives the clarified butter a distinctively nutty, caramelized flavor that is completely different from the pure butter flavor of Western clarified butter. Ghee has deep roots in Ayurvedic practices and is the cooking fat of choice in traditional Indian cooking. You won't find it in the butter case in your grocery store though—look for it with the cooking oils instead.

HOW TO KEEP BUTTER FRESH

Once you bring your butter home from the store, it'll keep in the fridge for about three months (check the expiration date on the package), and in the freezer for up to six months in its original store packaging. If you're wondering why butter can stay fresh for so long when your milk can't last longer than a week and your cheese gets moldy after a month, it's because butter has a higher fat content and lower water content than any other type of dairy product. Because of this, and because all butter these days is made with pasteurized cream, it is perfectly safe to keep butter in an airtight container on the counter for up to a week. Salt is a natural preservative (in the pre-pasteurization days butter was extremely salty in an effort to keep it fresh), so salted butter is the safer option to leave out at room temperature without risk of spoiling. Even modern butter will eventually go bad, though. It'll likely turn rancid due to oxidation before you'll see mold grow on it. If you're concerned if it's still fresh or not, give it a whiff: If it smells funky and overly sour, it's starting to spoil and it's time to say goodbye. If you can't tell by smell, taste it! Rancid butter is also a darker shade of yellow and has a greasier texture than fresh butter.

In my kitchen I keep a stick of salted cultured butter on the counter in an airtight dish for daily use, and more in the fridge for when that runs out. I always have at least a pound of unsalted butter in the fridge for baking with, plus extra in the freezer.

A DOZEN AND ONE THINGS
A BIT OF BUTTER INSTANTLY MAKES BETTER

Later in this book I focus on recipes made with a lot of butter, where the butter is integral to the food being made. But a knob (or pat, tablespoon, swipe, or curl) of butter can be equally transformative—add it to any of these foods for instant pleasure. Salted butter is best in these applications, but you can also add a sprinkle of salt on top of your unsalted butter.

1 **Toast** • There is nothing quite like the way butter melts through a piece of warm toast, turning it moist, infusing it with flavor—and eventually dripping down your fingers.

2 **Bread** • Good sliced, crusty bread slathered with enough room-temperature butter that your teeth leave marks in it with each bite is elemental. A slice of cold butter on a piece of bread is equally soul nourishing, and completely different.

3 **Pasta Sauce** • Anytime you're making pasta, no matter the sauce, add a bit of cold butter just before serving and stir it in until it's melted and combined. Tomato sauce, pesto, alla Norma, Bolognese, mac and cheese…butter makes them all better!

4   **Oatmeal** • A bowl of hot oatmeal (or any hot porridge) with a pat of butter melting in its center is like a warm hug on a chilly morning.

5   **Pancake Syrup** • Can you eat pancakes without butter on top? Of course not! Make them even better by melting a knob of butter into maple syrup and drizzling the hot mixture over your next stack—you'll never again do it any other way.

6   **Steamed Veggies** • Crisp-tender steamed peas, broccoli, asparagus, or green beans don't need anything more than a quick toss in a bit of salted butter to be ready to serve.

7   **Stale Muffins or Cake** • Boring or stale muffins or cake just need a bit of softened butter spread on them to be delicious again. Lay a buttered slice in a hot skillet to melt the butter and toast the cake for further improvement.

8   **Steak** • While that steak you just finished searing rests before slicing, plop a pat of butter on top of it and let it melt—it intensifies the flavor of the steak in a really nice way. Use a compound butter (page 48) instead to add a new flavor dimension.

9 **Eggs** • Soft-boiled eggs are best eaten out of the shell with a little spoon and a spoonful of butter tucked into the molten center. Scrambled eggs are best made in a skillet in a pool of melted butter.

10 **Rice** • Before you serve that pot of freshly steamed rice, add a slice or two of butter, then stir and fluff with a fork, and it'll be twice as nice.

11 **Baked Potatoes** • In case you missed it: Tucking into a hot baked potato with a pat of butter melting into it is one of life's most essential cozy pleasures.

12 **Corn on the Cob** • Whether you roll your cob across a stick or smear a pat across the rows with a butter knife, butter makes boiled corn on the cob sweeter, richer, and an all-American summertime classic.

13 **Sandwiches** • A layer of butter on each slice of bread adds moisture, richness, and flavor to any combination. Keep it simple with just thinly sliced ham and you've got France's favorite sandwich, the jambon-beurre. But don't stop there—try adding butter to your sandwich condiment lineup for any and every combination.

HOW TO MAKE CLARIFIED BUTTER

Also known as drawn butter, clarified butter is simply butter that has been melted, simmered, and strained to remove all the water and milk solids from it but none of the rich butter flavor. Unlike butter, which can burn and smoke and turn bitter when cooked at high temperatures, clarified butter has a higher smoke point, so it's better for high-heat cooking. I use it in my Pommes Anna (page 73) and for roasting vegetables, searing fish, and making hollandaise. Because it stays liquid longer than standard melted butter, it is the most elegant and delicious way to serve melted butter for dipping lobster or crab into. It's also amazing drizzled over hot homemade popcorn or any steamed veggie.

You can assume about 25 percent volume loss when turning butter into clarified butter. So, 1 cup of butter will give you about ¾ cup of clarified butter. You can store whatever you don't use right away in the fridge for several months, so don't worry about making extra.

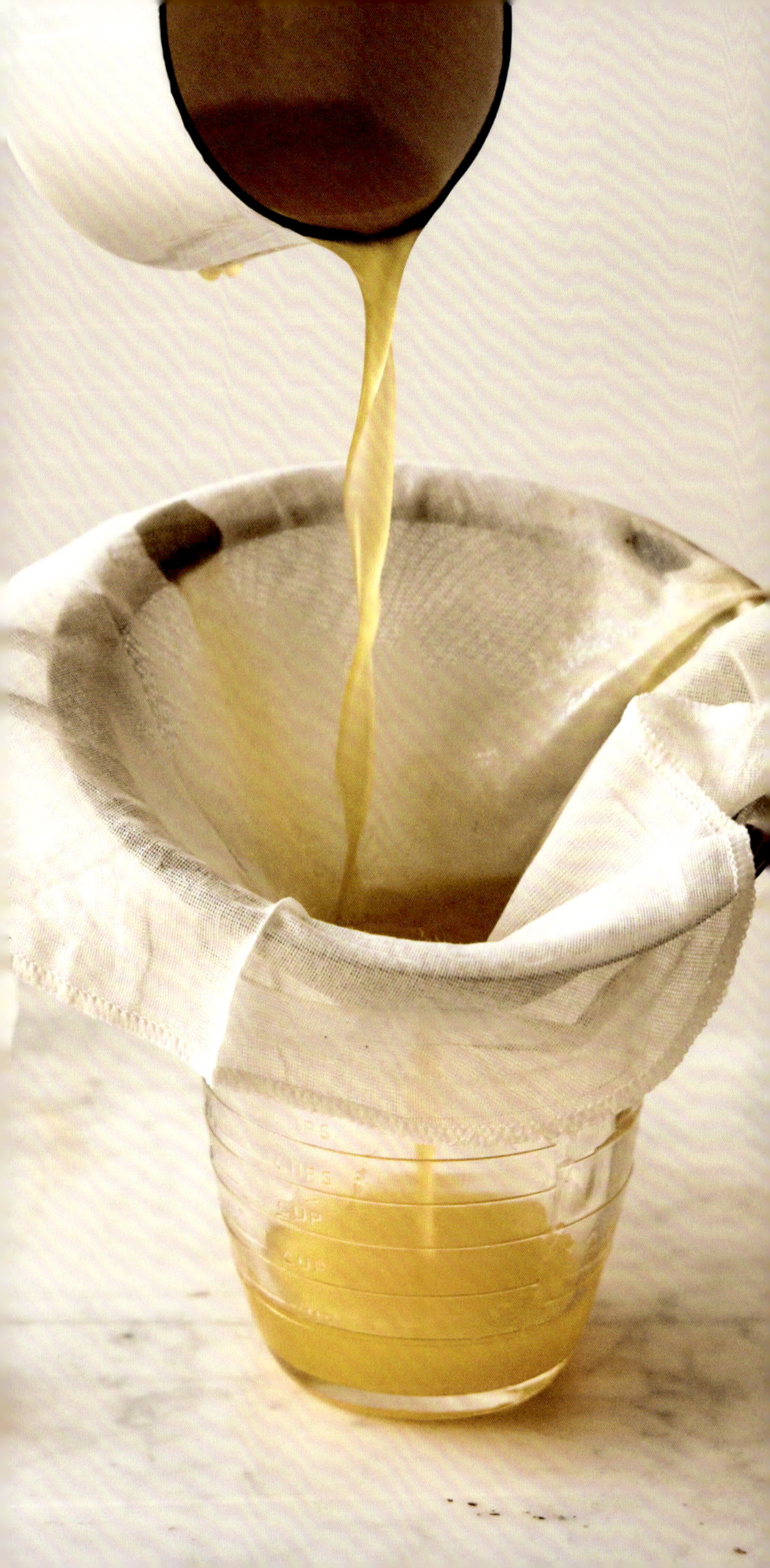

[TO MAKE CLARIFIED BUTTER]

1 • Place your butter in a medium saucepan over medium-low heat and let it melt, resisting the urge to stir or swirl. Once the butter has melted, it will begin to foam, and the solids will begin to sink to the bottom of the pan. Turn the heat down to low and let the butter continue to simmer for 10 minutes, then turn off the heat and skim the foam off the top with a spoon. Let the melted butter sit for 5 minutes.

2 • Place a sieve lined with cheesecloth or a coffee filter over a jar or bowl and pour the melted butter through. The milk solids will catch in the sieve, leaving your clarified butter in the jar. It is ready to cook with or enjoy right away. Store leftovers in an airtight container in the fridge for up to 3 months.

3 • Don't discard the milk solids, though— they're quite yummy. Spread them on a piece of bread and enjoy them while they're still warm or save them in the fridge and toss them into your next pasta dinner.

GHEE Ghee is a type of clarified butter that has been used for centuries in Indian cooking (page 38). To make your own ghee, use cultured, grass-fed butter to get the taste close to traditional ghee. Follow the same process for making clarified butter above but continue to simmer the butter until the milk solids at the bottom are dark brown and the melted fat is transparent and golden. This can take anywhere between 30 minutes and 1 hour, depending on how much butter you're working with.

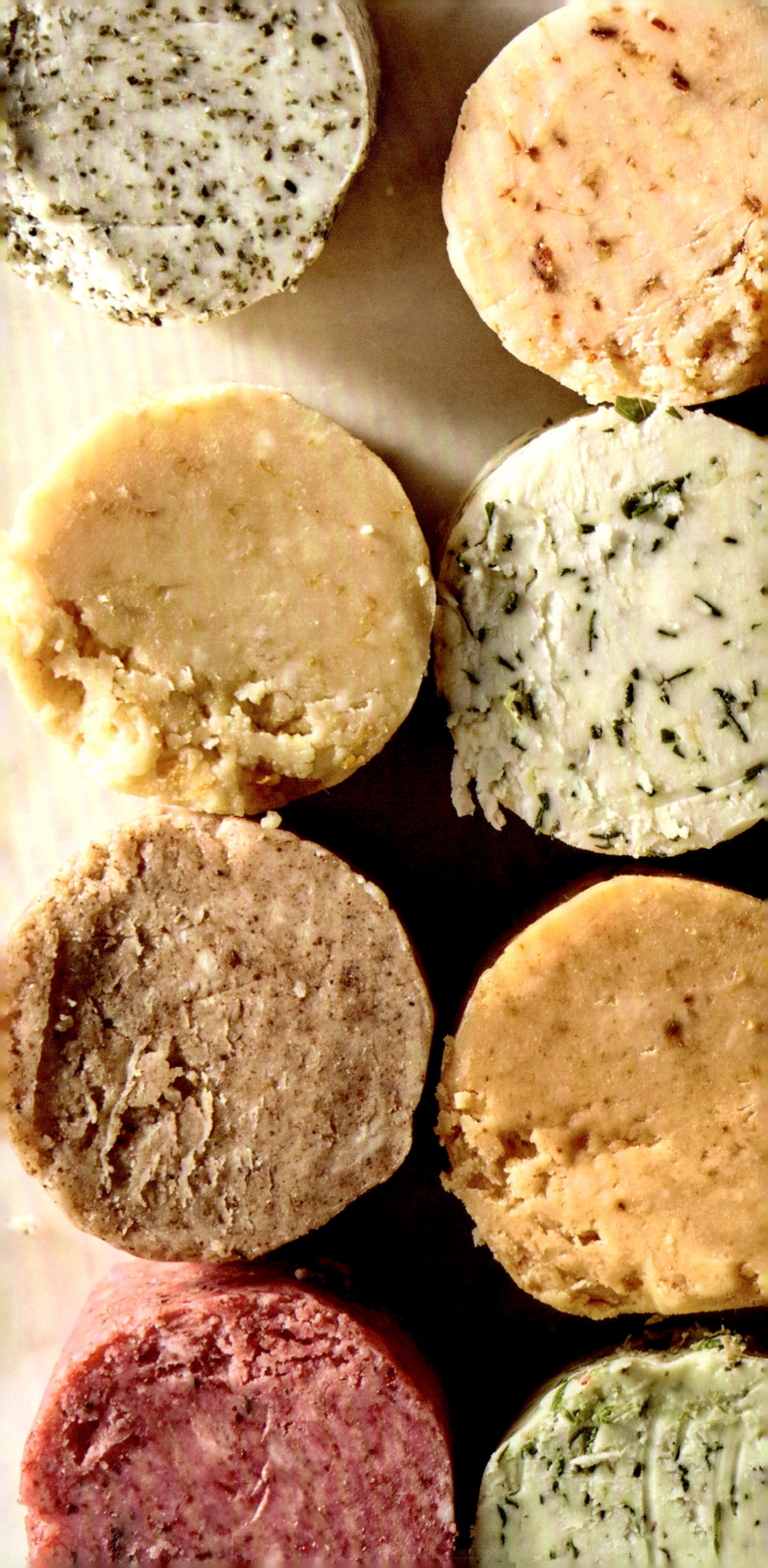

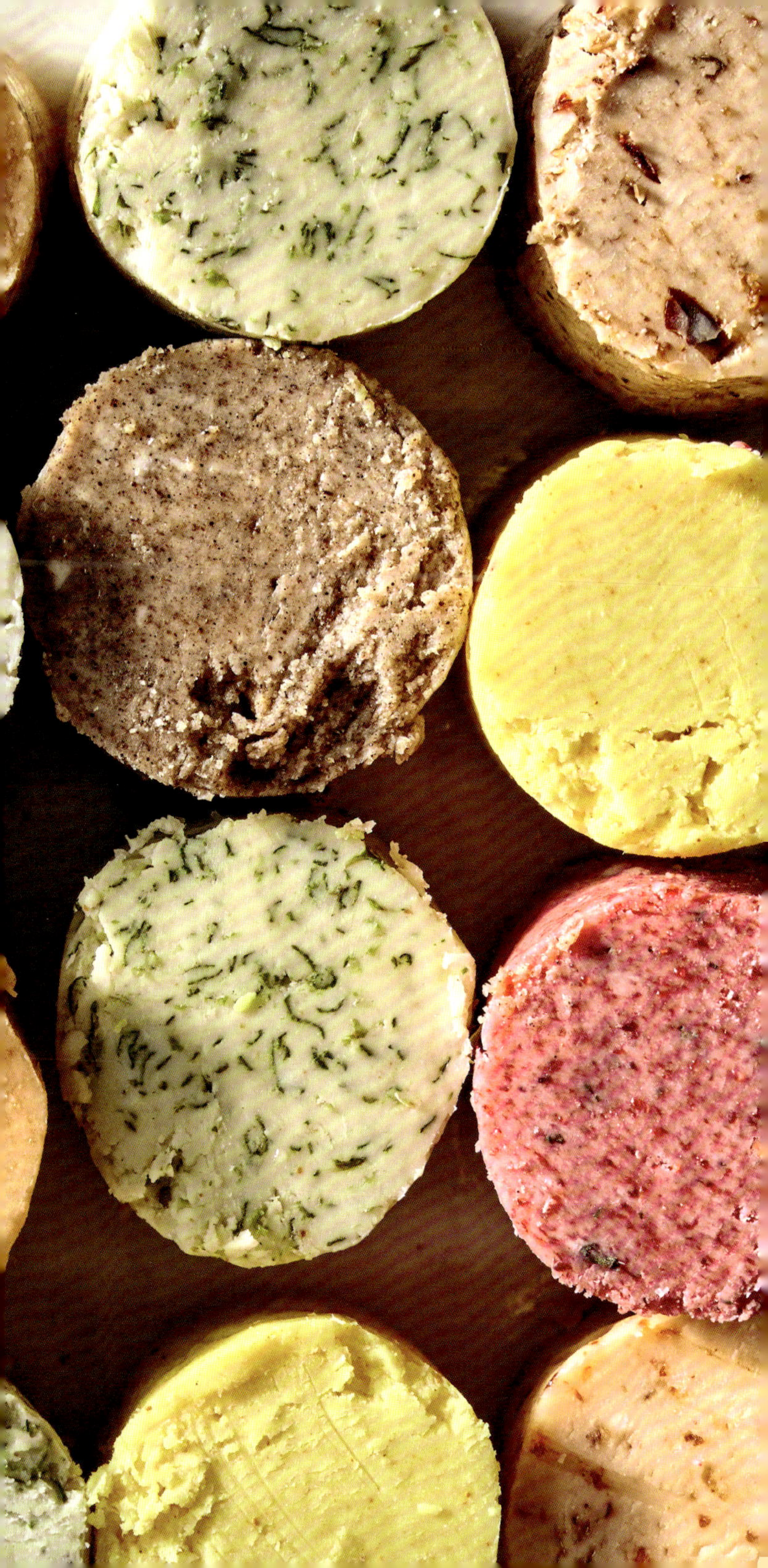

HOW TO MAKE COMPOUND BUTTER

When softened at room temperature or just after making, butter can be flavored with anything you can dream up, so long as that thing is not too liquidy. We call this kind of flavored butter compound butter, but your grandma might call it hotel butter. It's a make-ahead flavor shortcut that will make you feel like the most prepared and creative home cook in the world. Butter is a natural flavor carrier and amplifier, and compound butter does double time on both fronts. Add a pat of it on top of anything hot (steak, oatmeal, toast, roast fish, steamed green beans, etc.) and watch as it melts into an instant sauce. Use it to bake with, and your biscuits will be heaven scented. Serve a selection of compound butters with the bread at your next dinner party, and your guests won't shut up about it. Rub it all over a chicken before roasting for the most wonderfully seasoned and moist meal. Toss some pasta in compound butter and call it dinner.

The more rolls of compound butter you have sitting in your freezer or fridge, the richer you are in flavor. I've listed a dozen of my favorite recipes for compound butter in the chart on pages 50–51, but you don't have to stop there.

[TO MAKE COMPOUND BUTTER]

1 • Start with 1 stick of butter that has gotten nice and soft at room temperature, or with ½ cup [113 g] of freshly kneaded homemade butter. Mash it around in a medium bowl with a silicone spatula or wooden spoon and stir in your mix-ins until they're well incorporated. Taste and adjust the seasoning as needed.

2 • You can serve your compound butter immediately by transferring it to a small bowl, but the flavor intensifies if it has a chance to chill. Transfer the butter mixture to a piece of parchment paper, patting it into a sort of log shape toward one long end of the parchment. Pull the parchment paper up and over the butter, then roll it tightly into a uniform cylinder about 1½ inches [4 cm] wide, twisting the parchment in opposite directions at each end (like an old-fashioned candy wrapper) to secure. Chill until firm.

3 • Compound butter keeps in the fridge for up to 2 weeks, or in the freezer for a few months—just seal your parchment-wrapped rolls in a freezer bag before freezing.

FOR ½ CUP [113 G] OF ROOM TEMPERATURE, UNSALTED BUTTER, ADD:

SEAWEED BUTTER	MAÎTRE D' HÔTEL BUTTER	CILANTRO-LIME BUTTER	GREEN GODDESS BUTTER	PUTTANESCA BUTTER	SMOKY GARLIC BUTTER
Great on steak, toast, and eggs!	The original French compound butter, it's très bien on anything.	I love it on corn on the cob or chicken.	Dip radishes and bread in it or melt it over a baked potato.	Add it to your pasta or use it on roasted white fish.	Roast chicken with it or toss steamed green beans in it.
1 Tbsp dried kelp flakes	1 Tbsp finely chopped parsley	1 Tbsp finely chopped cilantro	1 anchovy fillet, finely chopped	1 anchovy fillet, finely chopped	1 garlic clove, finely grated
¼ tsp kosher salt	1 tsp lemon juice	1 tsp finely grated lime zest	1 Tbsp finely chopped parsley	1 tsp capers, finely chopped	½ tsp smoked paprika
	½ tsp finely grated lemon zest	1 tsp lime juice	1 Tbsp finely chopped tarragon	1 tsp tomato powder	½ tsp kosher salt
	½ tsp kosher salt	½ tsp kosher salt	2 tsp finely chopped chives	½ tsp crushed red pepper flakes	
		¼ tsp cayenne	¼ tsp freshly ground black pepper	⅛ tsp kosher salt	
			¼ tsp kosher salt		
[1]	[2]	[3]	[4]	[5]	[6]

TYPE | USE | INGREDIENTS

TYPE	**USE**	**INGREDIENTS**
MISO-ORANGE BUTTER	*Excellent on any white fish and delicious baked into biscuits!*	1 Tbsp finely grated orange zest 1 Tbsp white miso paste ¼ tsp kosher salt [7]
HOT HONEY BUTTER	*Cozy on toast, but happier when glazing shrimp.*	1 Tbsp honey 1 tsp Aleppo-style chili flakes ¼ tsp kosher salt [8]
GOLDEN BUTTER	*Bake with it for extra spice or melt it over chicken.*	2 tsp finely grated fresh ginger 1 tsp granulated sugar ½ tsp turmeric ½ tsp freshly ground black pepper ¼ tsp kosher salt [9]
RASPBERRY-THYME BUTTER	*Fun on bread, but extra special mixed into frosting for cake.*	¼ cup [5 g] dehydrated raspberries, pulverized into a powder in the food processor 1 tsp finely chopped fresh thyme ½ tsp granulated sugar ¼ tsp kosher salt [10]
PUMPKIN SPICE BUTTER	*Turns toast into pumpkin spice toast, and bakes well into biscuits.*	2 tsp pumpkin spice 2 tsp granulated sugar ¼ tsp kosher salt [11]
VANILLA BEAN BUTTER	*Serve it on bread with anchovies à la Saint Julivert Fisherie—trust me.*	2 tsp granulated sugar 1½ tsp vanilla bean seeds ¼ tsp kosher salt [12]

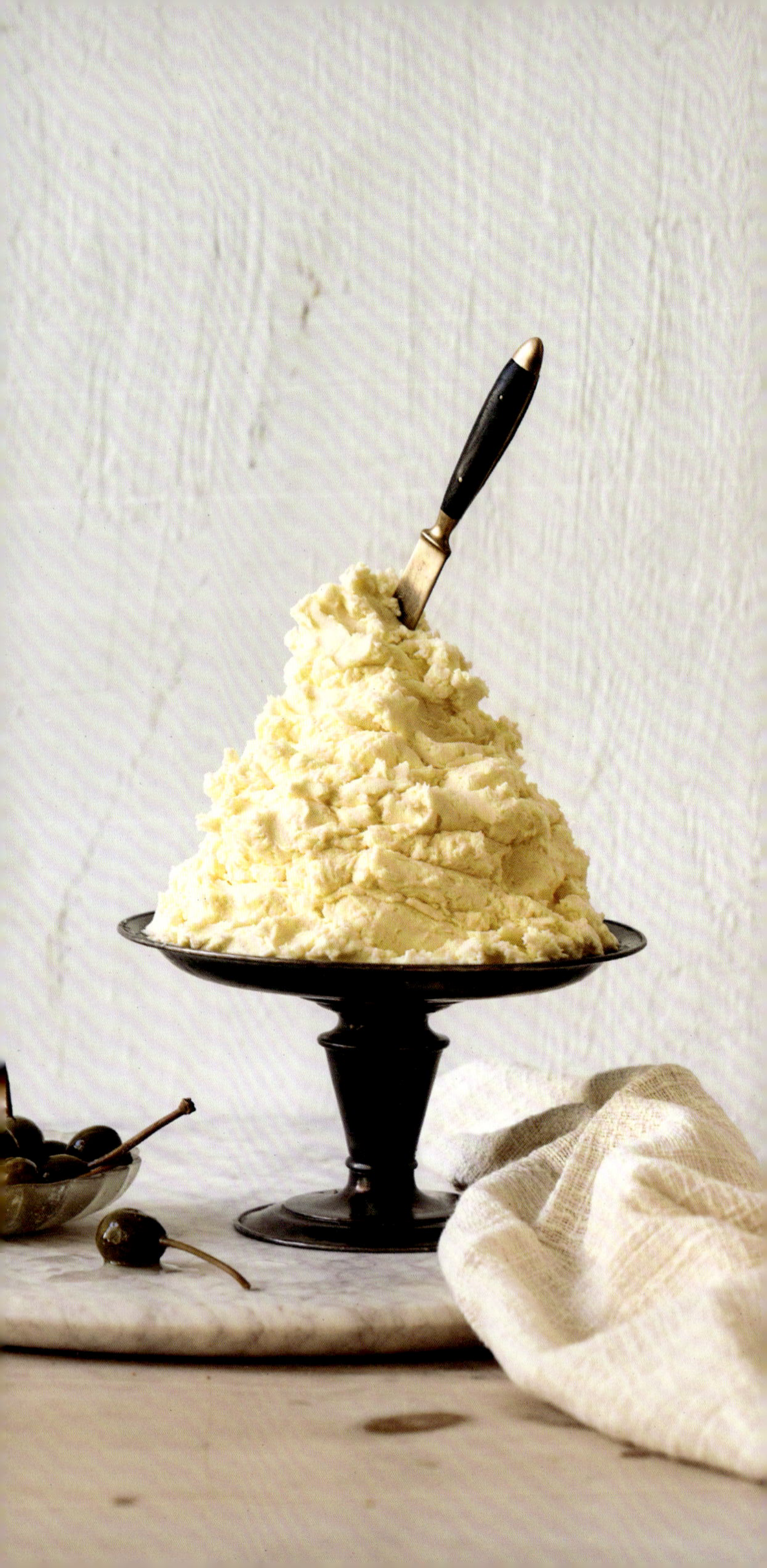

HOW TO MAKE WHIPPED BUTTER

At many restaurants, especially those with a retro flair, the bread basket arrives with a ramekin of fluffy whipped butter piped in a rosette. Beating air into softened butter increases the volume of the butter and makes it easier to spread over bread. Some people whip a little water or milk into the butter during this process to further increase the volume of the butter or add oil, which makes the butter easily spreadable when cold (this is what that "butter spread" you see in the grocery store is—butter blended with oil so that it remains spreadable straight from the fridge).

I add heavy cream to my whipped butter, and I think you should too. It gives you whipped butter that is halfway between a spread and a dip, feels lighter and fluffier than butter, and tastes oh so creamy. Drizzle honey over the top and serve it with freshly baked biscuits.

Swirl it into a bowl and surround it with radishes and cucumbers for dipping. Or if you're feeling fancy, pipe it into rosettes, chill them, and then use them to top stacks of hot pancakes, serve with bread, or top baked potatoes—it'll be better than at any fancy restaurant.

[TO MAKE WHIPPED BUTTER]

---

1 • Start with room-temperature butter in the bowl of a stand mixer fitted with the paddle attachment. I like to use a good-quality sweet cream butter for this, nothing cultured or too grassy. For every 1 stick of butter (½ cup [113 g]), add 2 Tbsp of heavy cream.

---

2 • Beat the butter, starting on the lowest setting and working your way up to the highest once the cream is incorporated, until it's light and fluffy, about a minute or two. Stop halfway through to scrape down the sides of the bowl. Season to taste with salt and beat to combine. That's it!

MAKE A BUTTER MOUNTAIN It's recently become a thing in hip restaurants to display a big mound of softened butter from which servers scoop lavish amounts to accompany bread service. It's all about the spectacle, the ritual, and the bounty. Next time you have a party, make your own butter mountain and serve it surrounded by a field of bread. Soften some butter (a lot of butter) or, better yet, make a big batch of whipped butter, then scoop and mound and swirl it up on a plate until it's as tall as you can make it. Stick a knife in it—it's done.

HOW TO SOFTEN BUTTER

Softened butter should be easily mushed and squished but not greasy or melting. The best way to get to this perfectly soft texture is to let the butter sit at room temperature for at least 2 hours (though don't let it sit for more than 24 hours). If you need to speed up the process, avoid the microwave—the risk is great that you will end up with butter that's part melted and part hard. Instead, cut the butter into small pieces and lay it out on a plate in a warm (but not too hot) spot in your kitchen for about 30 minutes.

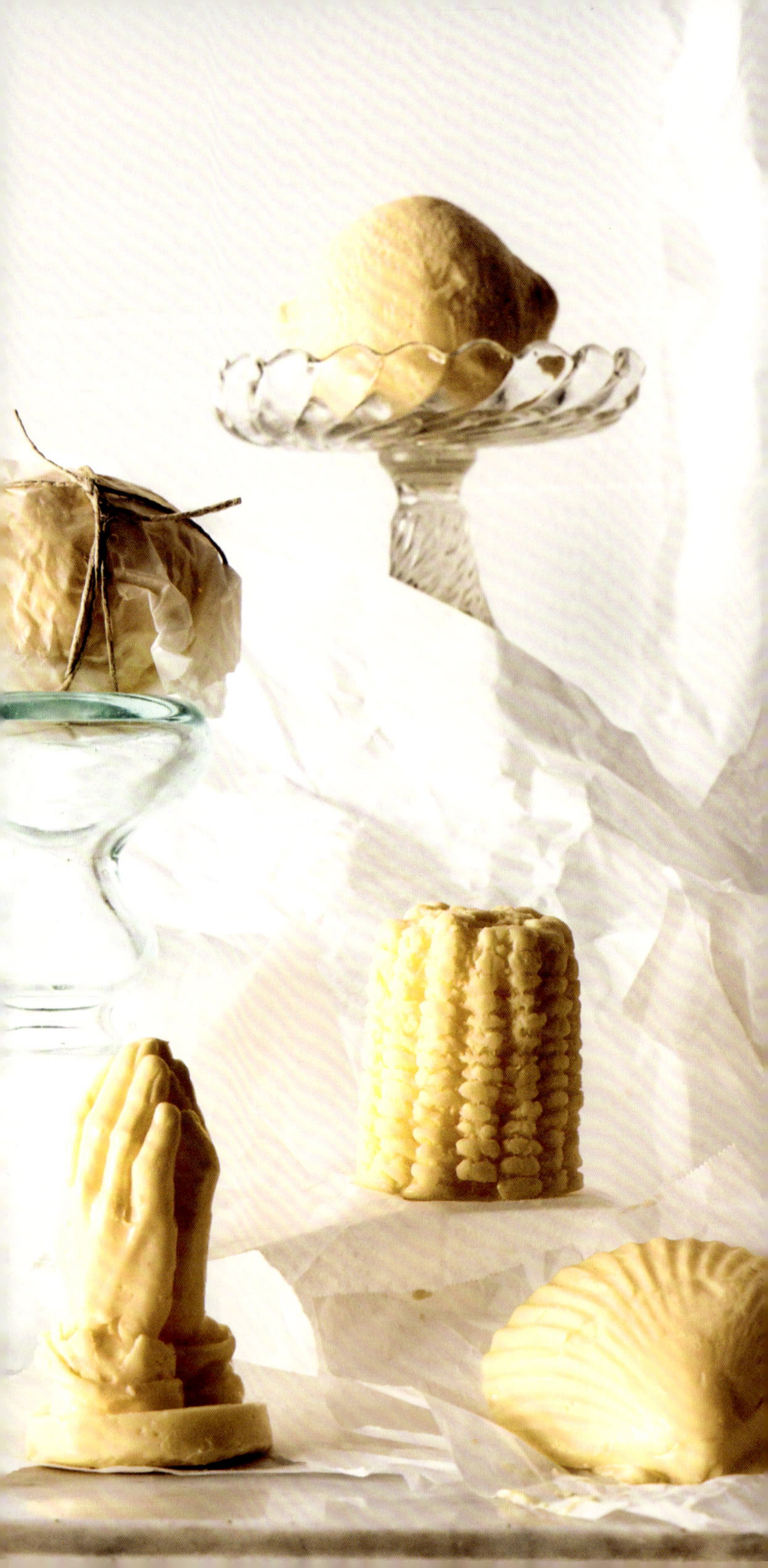

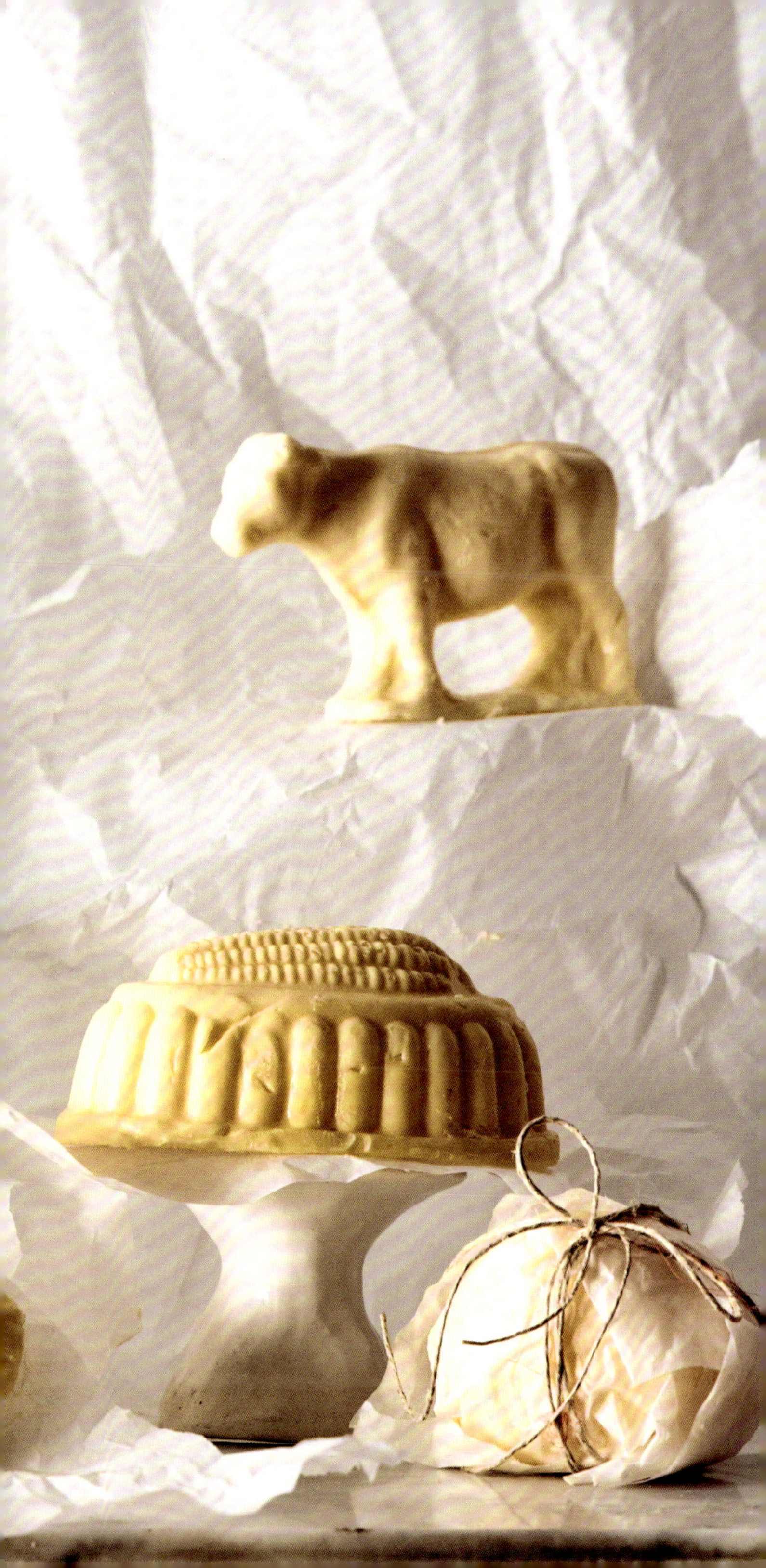

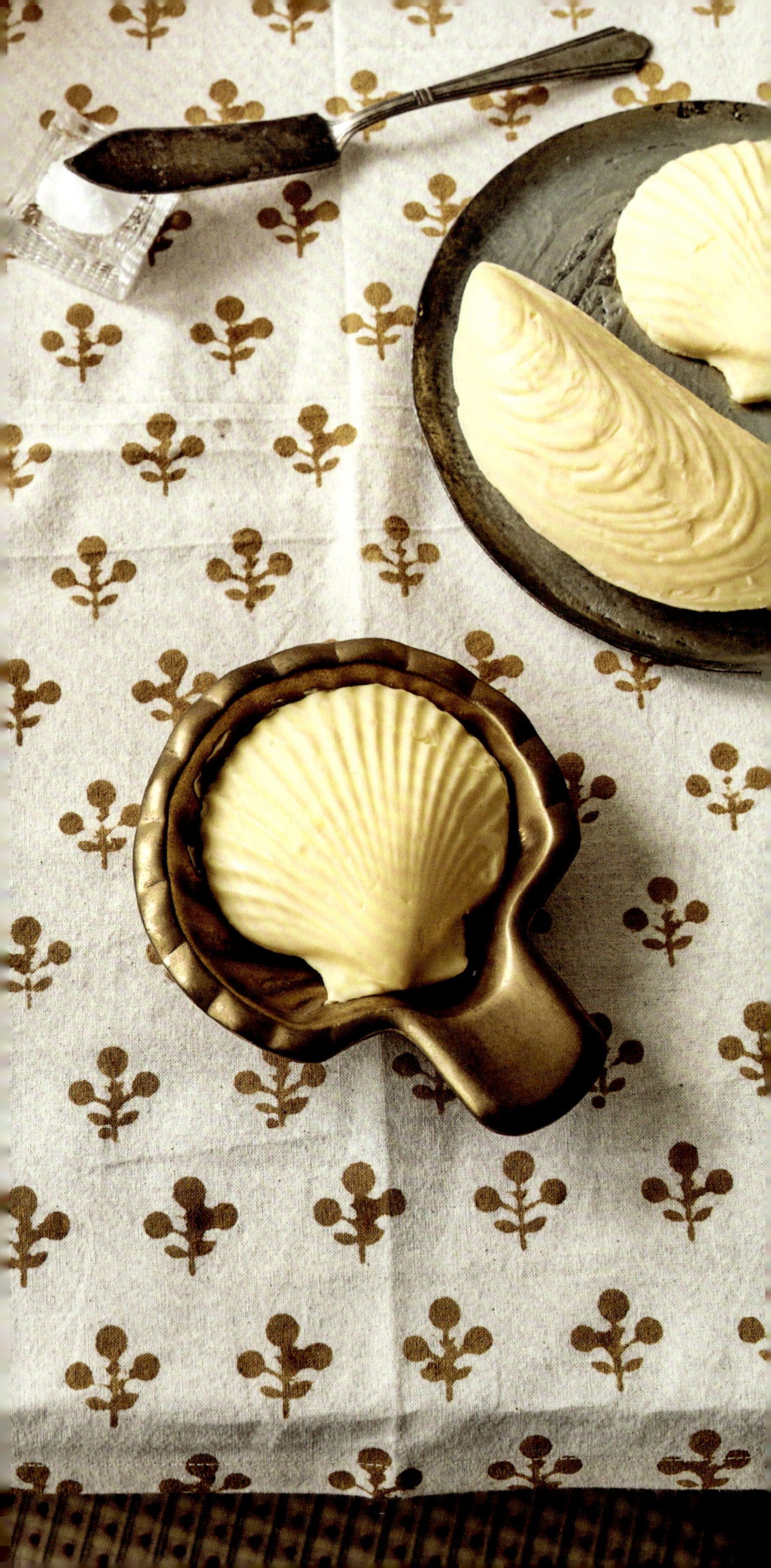

BUTTER SCULPTURES
AND OTHER FUN WAYS TO SERVE BUTTER

As long as humans have been making butter, we've been decorating it. The first documented use of a butter sculpture is from a 1536 dinner party in Rome, where chef Bartolomeo Scappi carved Hercules with a lion as the centerpiece of the banquet table. Through the European Renaissance and Baroque periods, butter sculptures could be found in the ballrooms and great halls of nobility putting on a show for their guests. Meanwhile, farmwives making homemade butter to sell at market developed unique ways to mark their butter by pressing a pattern into each block with hand-carved wooden presses. By the eighteenth century, smaller-scale decorative butter pats were the norm on English dinner tables. In the United States, to this day, public art butter sculptures at state fairs celebrate local dairy industries. It all started with a life-size butter cow at the Iowa State Fair in 1911, and it's been happening ever since—but what bothers me about state fair butter sculptures is they're not meant to be eaten! Besides those sculptures, decorative butter sort of fell out of favor in the Western world by the late nineteenth century, due to several factors including the margarine takeover, dairy production leaving the farm for the factories, and wartime rationing.

Luckily for you and me, we are now in a new butter renaissance, and it's time to celebrate it by decorating and molding some butter for your table. You don't need to go full-on Baroque banquet art or even carve anything at all to inspire and delight with edible butter sculptures.

[TO MAKE BUTTER SCULPTURES]

Use Silicone Molds
You can find a silicone mold online for almost any shape you can dream of making. Don't search for a "silicone butter mold," though, as that won't get you far. Instead search for a "silicone lemon shaped candle mold," or a "silicone shell shaped candy mold," or maybe a "silicone corn cob shaped resin mold." Whether they're marketed for making candles, candy, fondant, resin, or soap, a silicone mold works great for making a butter sculpture—just check that it's food-safe.

To use a silicone mold, get your butter nice and soft at room temperature, then use a rubber spatula to spread and squish and mash it into the silicone mold, making sure to press the butter into all the edges and crevices. Cover the exposed butter with parchment paper and pop it in the freezer for at least two hours and up to two months. The day you plan to serve it, unmold the frozen butter sculpture by pressing it out while you pull the mold inside out. Let your sculpture come to room temperature for a couple hours before serving.

Use a Vintage Wooden Butter Press or Mold

The world is full of these darling tools from every decade—keep your eyes open for them on your next flea market jaunt or start searching eBay and soon you might just find yourself with a whole collection. You can also still buy new ones, usually made in Germany or France. There are three different kinds you'll find: simple carved and decorated troughs to press butter into; slightly more advanced ones that include a plunger to press the molded butter out of the mold; and molds made in multiple parts with hinges and latches to surround a block of butter like a springform pan (these press designs into all sides, then easily release once they're set). All these versions come in many different shapes and sizes, holding anywhere from a pat to a pound of butter.

To use a wooden butter mold, first, make sure it's nice and clean. Then soak it in ice water for 20 minutes before filling it with room-temperature butter. Use a rubber spatula to press the butter in firmly. Chill it (in the mold!) in the fridge until firm (about 1 hour), and then release it from the mold.

Use Two-Piece Candy Molds

Before there were silicone molds for making 3D confections, there were two-part plastic, metal, or even wood candy molds. Think classic chocolate Easter Bunnies and Santas. These work great for making butter sculptures. Sometimes they're even marketed as butter molds, especially when they're in the shape of a lamb, cow, or turkey. You can find them in cake and baking stores, or search online for a "two-part 3D candy mold" in the shape you desire.

To use a candy mold, fill each half with softened butter, using a rubber spatula to squish the butter into every little corner of the mold. It's best if the mold is clear so you can see if the butter is coming in full contact with the mold or not. Scrape off any excess butter, then fit the two halves together and squish to seal. Make sure the edges of each side are lining up as neatly as possible. Freeze for at least 2 hours (and up to 2 months). The day you plan to serve it, unmold the frozen butter sculpture by pulling the two sides of the mold apart. You'll need to do a little cosmetic cleanup work with a paring knife to shave off any seam lines, then let your sculpture come to room temperature before serving.

Make Butter Curls

Despite my hate for single-use tools, I am now the proud owner of two butter curlers (page 29). I find it deeply satisfying to make butter curls. Before you start curling, fill one bowl with very hot water and a second bowl with ice water. Dunk your butter curler into the hot water and then pull it down the length of a stick of cold butter to make ribbonlike curls. If the ribbons aren't curling up enough, give them a little guidance with your hands, then immediately tuck them into the ice bath so that they hold their shape until you're ready to serve them.

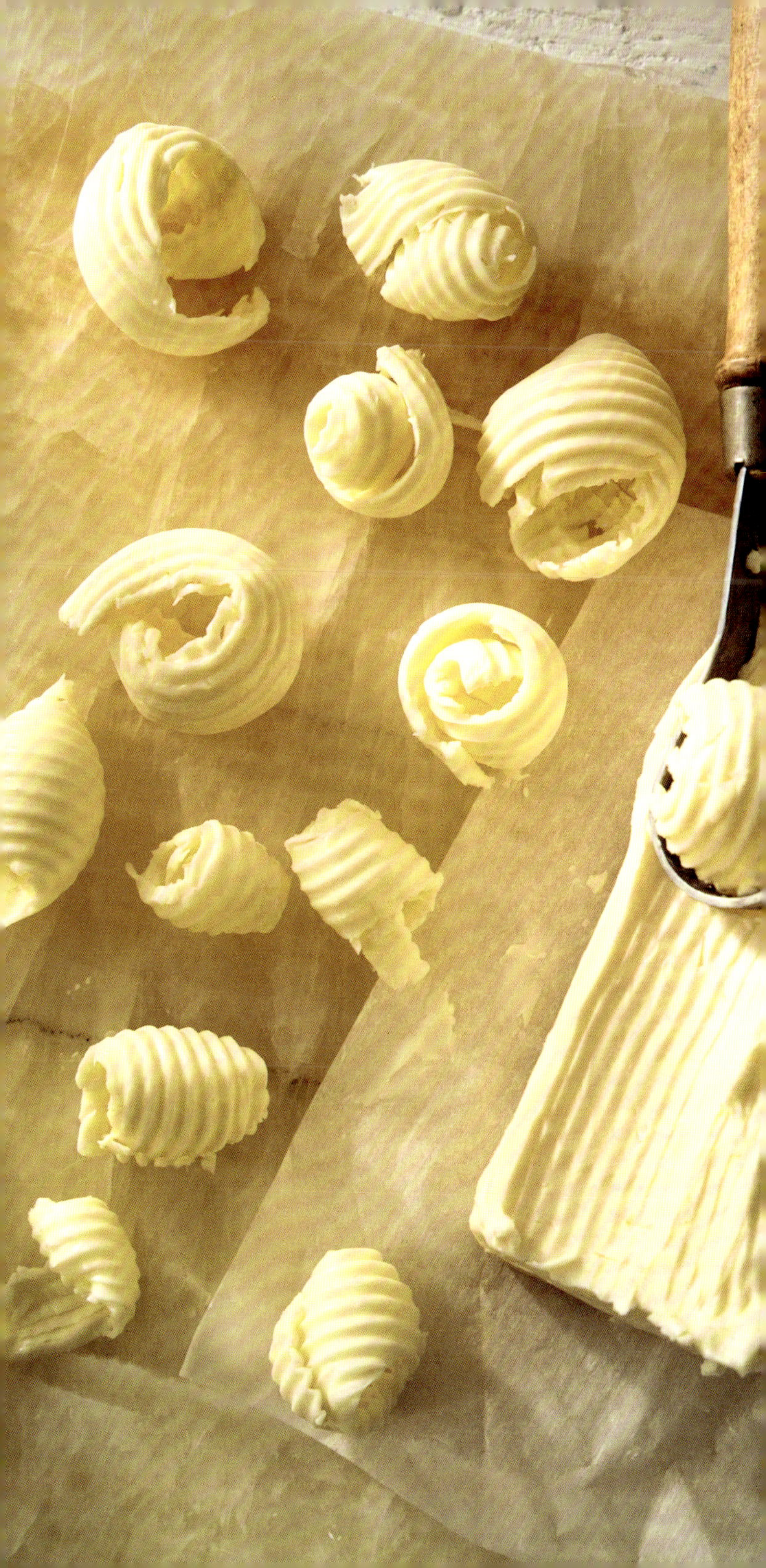

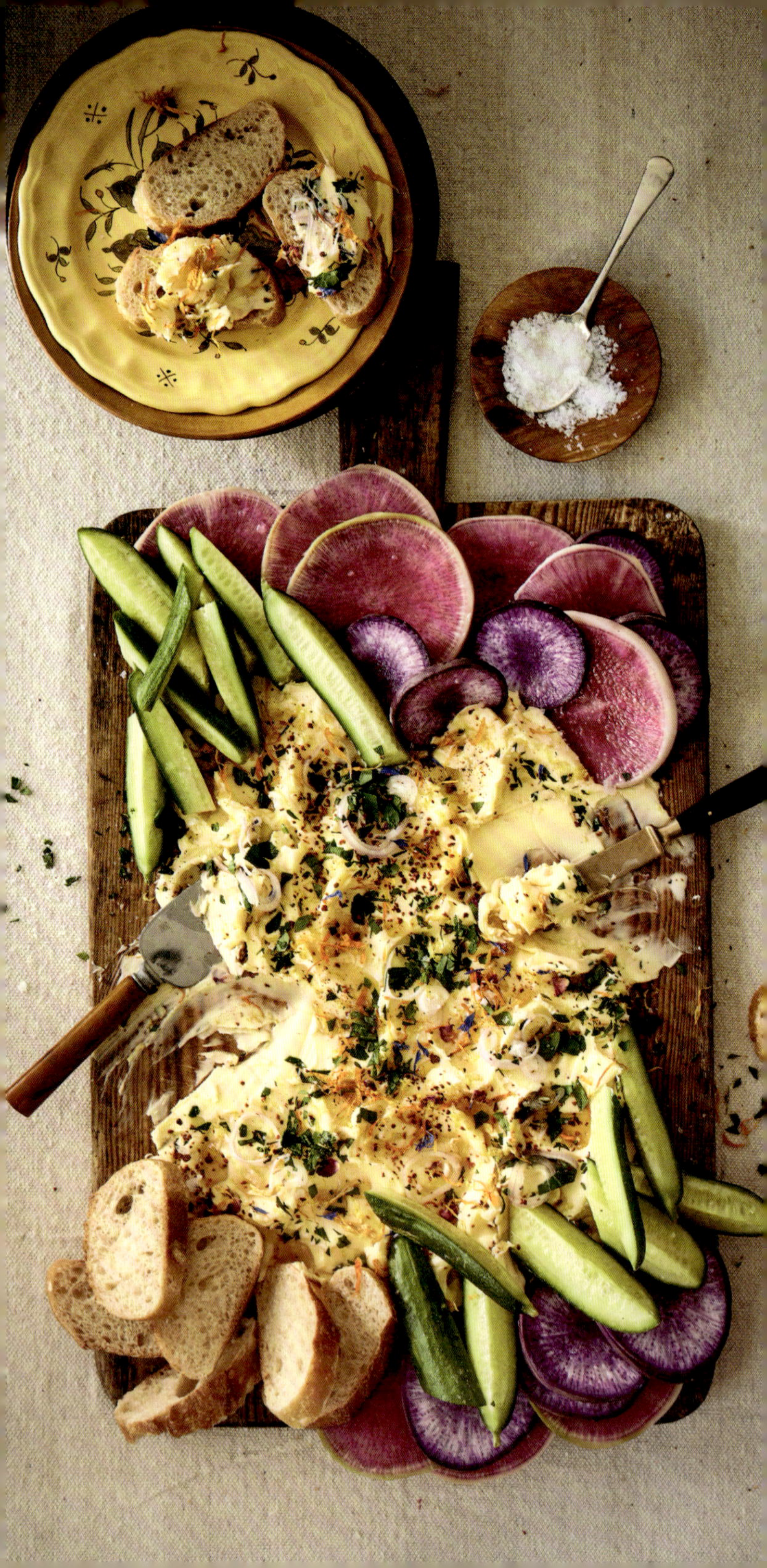

BUTTER BOARDS
FOR EASY ENTERTAINING

In the fall of 2022, #butterboard started taking over food TikTok and then Instagram after Justine Doiron posted a video of making a butter board inspired by a recipe in Joshua McFadden's cookbook *Six Seasons*. This came after what felt like years of elaborate charcuterie board arrangements filling every social media feed. The butter board was cheaper to make but still an inviting canvas on which to display colorful creativity at cocktail hour, and influencers couldn't stop making them. The idea is simple: Spread softened butter over the surface of a board (or plate or platter), top it with a bunch of pretty things that add flavor and texture, then eat it by swiping pieces of bread right through it. It's easy to make, it's communal, it's showy, it's fun, and it involves eating with your hands—all the things I love in food. And yet, I was initially skeptical because of how trendy it was. The fad has calmed down now, but it hasn't gone away, and honestly it shouldn't—butter boards are a great trick for easy entertaining. I'm fully on board with them, now and forever.

[TO MAKE A BUTTER BOARD]

---

1 • Start with your favorite high-quality salted butter at room temperature. You'll want about ¼ cup (55 g) of butter per guest. It'll need to sit out for at least 2 hours to get nice and soft, longer if it's cold in your kitchen, so plan accordingly.

---

2 • Pick a board, slate, marble cheese slab, or even a platter—the bigger the guest list, the bigger the board—and make sure you wash it very well and dry it. (Please don't use the cutting board you used to cut that raw chicken on yesterday.)

---

3 • Use a butter knife or spoon to scoop and dollop soft butter across the surface of your board, leaving an empty space around the edge of the board for your bread. Use the back of the spoon or the side of the knife to spread the dollops together into a single textured and swirly layer. You don't want the butter to be flat—it holds the toppings better with peaks and valleys.

---

4 • Now comes the fun part: the toppings! Start with a sprinkle of flaky sea salt and a grating of fresh citrus zest, and then follow your heart's desire with any combination of spices, chopped fresh herbs, chopped fruit or veggies, chopped olives, chopped anchovies, edible flower petals, jam, honey, nuts, seeds, etc. The only rule is it all needs to be cut up small enough to spread onto a piece of bread with the butter. The board doesn't have to be all the same: Go for pockets of sweet and savory, deep and fresh. Have one side spicy and one side sweet. Whatever toppings you choose, shower them over the butter board in a loose, artful scatter. Let your flavor-blending skills and creativity shine!

---

5 • To serve, arrange slices of crusty bread around the edge of the board for dipping in the butter. Add a few butter knives if you'd like to be a bit more civilized. Add slices of watermelon radish, daikon, or cucumbers in addition to or instead of the bread if you prefer—they're equally good spread with dolled-up butter.

TEN FAVORITE RECIPES THAT DEPEND ON BUTTER

It's easy to love butter as a spread or a finishing touch, but more than anything, I love cooking and baking with butter. It's an essential structural building block and flavor powerhouse. It's a sauce emulsifier, a taste enhancer, and a bringer of joy. Because of the unique constitution of butter as a matrix of fats, water, and milk solids, it is an amazingly multitalented culinary catalyst. The temperature of butter and the way it is incorporated into other ingredients matters, and it changes everything. I could write many cookbooks focused on butter. What follows merely scratches the surface of some of the amazing things butter can do in your kitchen, with some of my favorite recipes that rely on, and shine with the flavor of, butter.

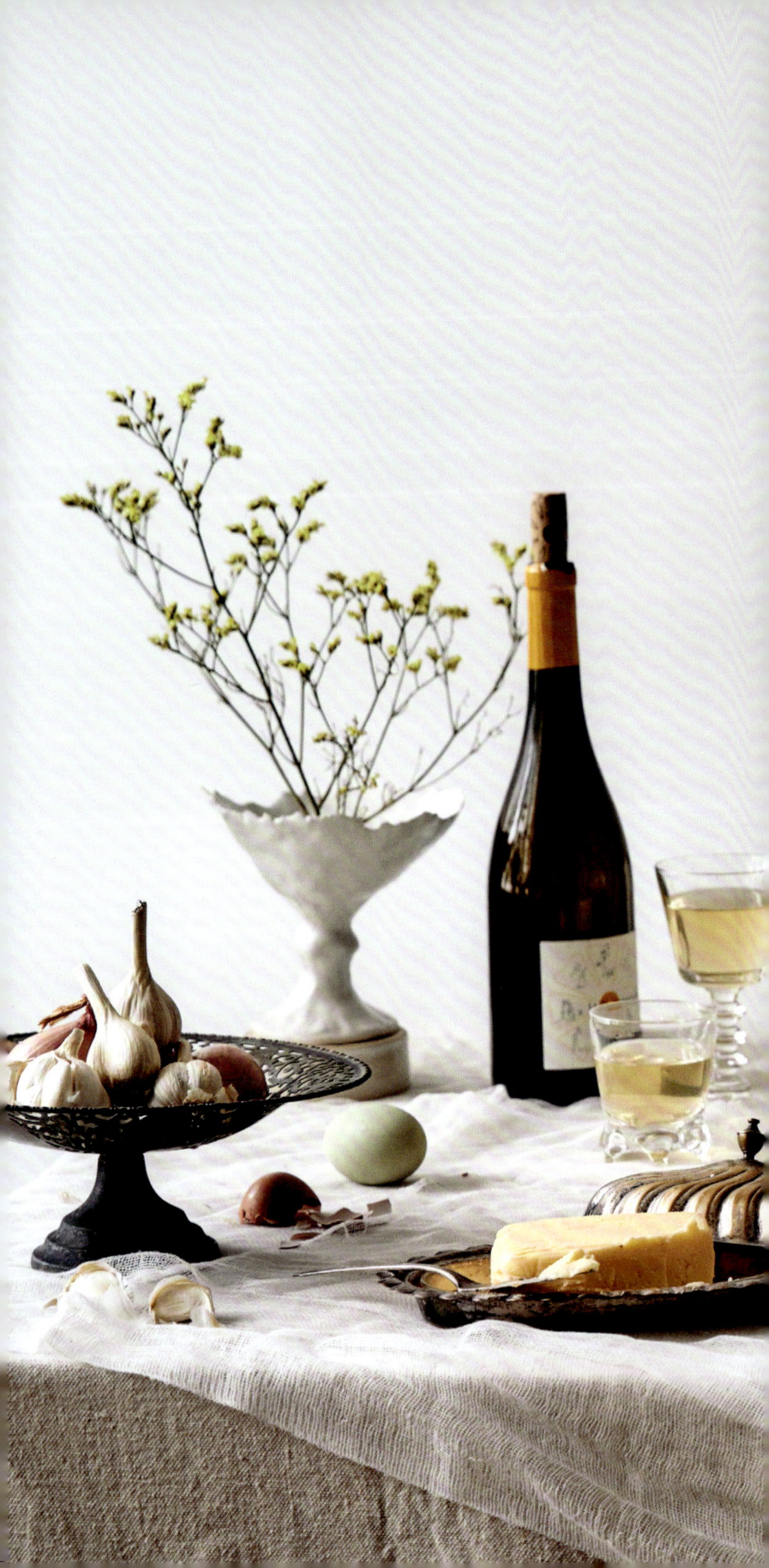

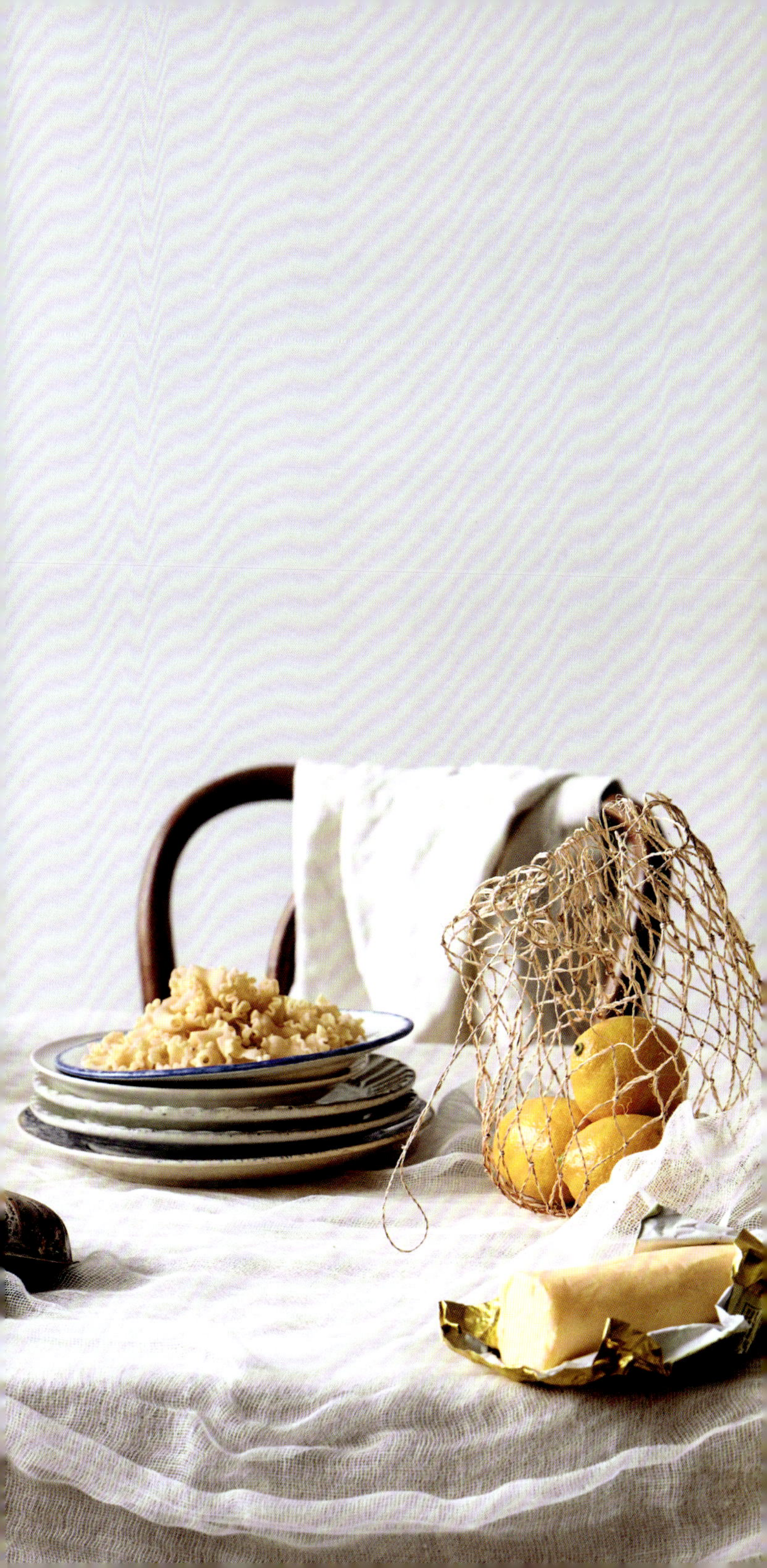

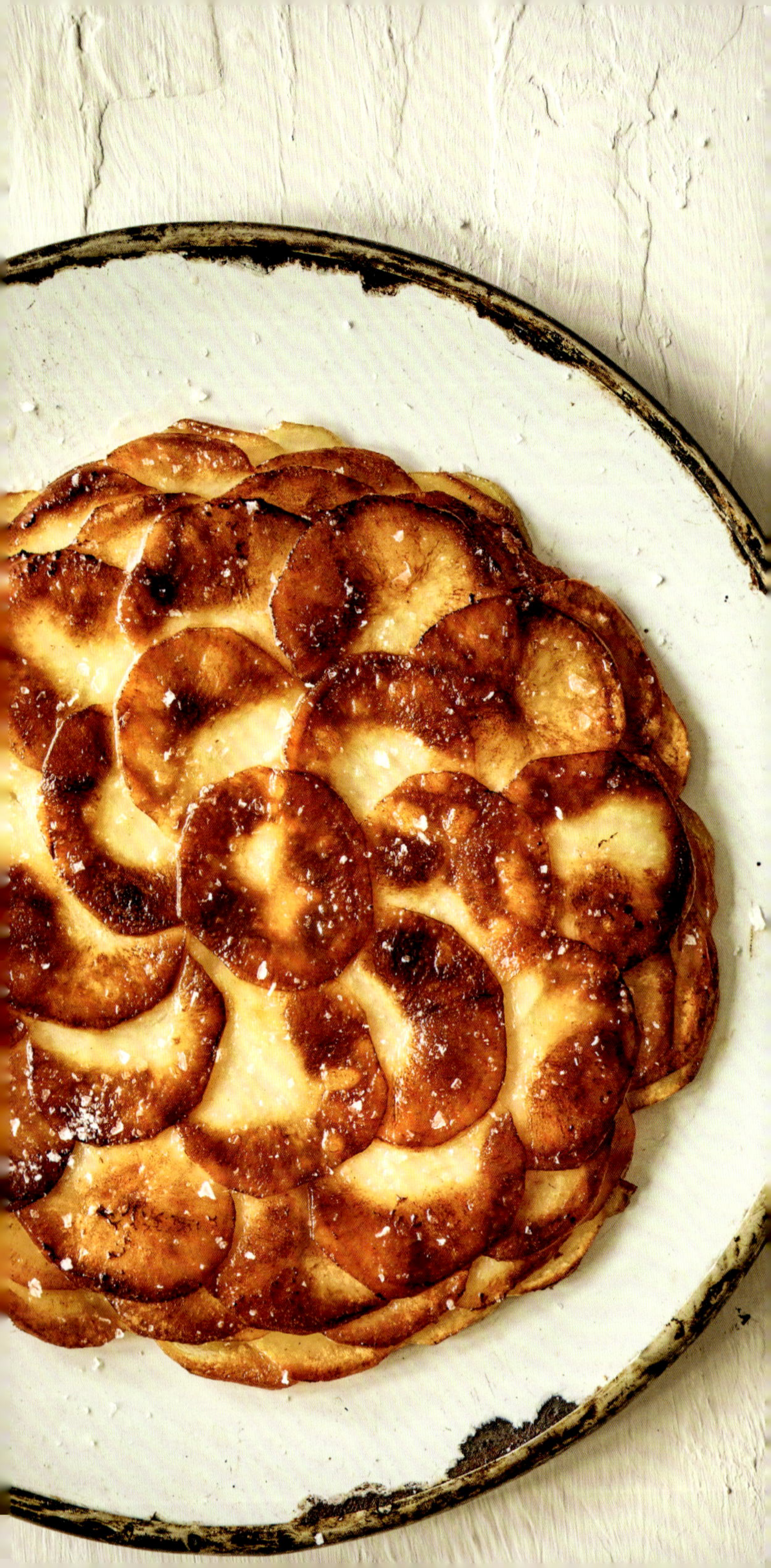

POMMES ANNA (À LA ANNA)

1½ lbs [680 g] (about 4 medium) russet potatoes

½ cup [120 ml] clarified butter (page 43), warmed

Kosher salt

SERVES 4

This is my favorite of all the classic French combinations of potatoes and butter. And not just because we share a name—I'm completely obsessed with the contrast between the shatteringly crisp crust and the tender buttery interior. It's a showy little side dish, one to pull out for company or a special occasion. (Fitting, since the dish was supposedly named after a gorgeous nineteenth-century French courtesan.) There are many slightly different ways to make Pommes Anna; the more traditional, the fussier the recipe gets. For my way, I cut a few corners without sacrificing any flavor. But the corner I'd never cut is using a generous amount of clarified butter to cook the potatoes—the fate of your Pommes Anna depends upon it. Clarified butter won't burn at high temperatures, so it's the perfect ingredient to crisp the potatoes and infuse them with rich flavor. You can use a very hot skillet in a very hot oven without any risk of bitter charring.

[INSTRUCTIONS]

1 Preheat the oven to 400°F [200°C].

2 Peel the potatoes and place them in a bowl of room-temperature water. Working with one at a

time, use a mandoline to slice the potatoes about
1/16 in [1.5 mm] thick into a large mixing bowl.
If you don't have a mandoline, you can use the
slicing blade of a food processor or carefully slice
by hand with a sharp knife. But a mandoline is
the best, fastest, and easiest way, and if you get
yourself a cut-proof glove to wear while you use
it, you'll never slice a fingertip off in the process,
I promise.

3   Pour about ¼ cup [55 g] of the butter over the
potato slices, season generously with salt, and
toss with your hands, making sure all the slices are
coated. The butter may start to seize and firm up
as it cools on the potatoes. Don't worry: That's
normal. Just try to get all the slices coated.

4   Swirl 2 Tbsp of the clarified butter in a 10 in
[25 cm] ovenproof nonstick skillet or well-
seasoned cast-iron skillet over medium-low heat.
Starting in the middle of the skillet, arrange the
potato slices in overlapping concentric circles
until the full surface is covered. Repeat to create a
second layer of potato circles.

5   Now, stop fussing—the first two are the
only layers anyone will ever see! Quickly and
haphazardly layer the rest of the potato slices
into the skillet. Use a spatula to press and pat
the potatoes down into a firm, flat cake. Pour the
remaining butter over the top and around the
edges of the potatoes, cover, and increase the
heat to medium. Cook, covered and undisturbed,
for 5 minutes. Uncover, press and pat the
potatoes down with a spatula again, then give
the skillet a wiggle to make sure the potato slices
are sticking together and not to your pan. If the
potato pancake doesn't slide as one unit at this

point, cover the skillet and continue to cook, checking every 2 minutes, until it does.

6 Transfer to the oven and bake, uncovered, for 15 to 20 minutes, until you can see the edges are deeply golden brown and a cake tester or sharp knife glides easily when inserted into the center.

7 Holding the potato pancake in place with a spatula, pour off and discard the excess butter from the skillet, then invert the pancake onto a serving platter or cutting board. Let sit for 5 minutes before slicing into wedges to serve.

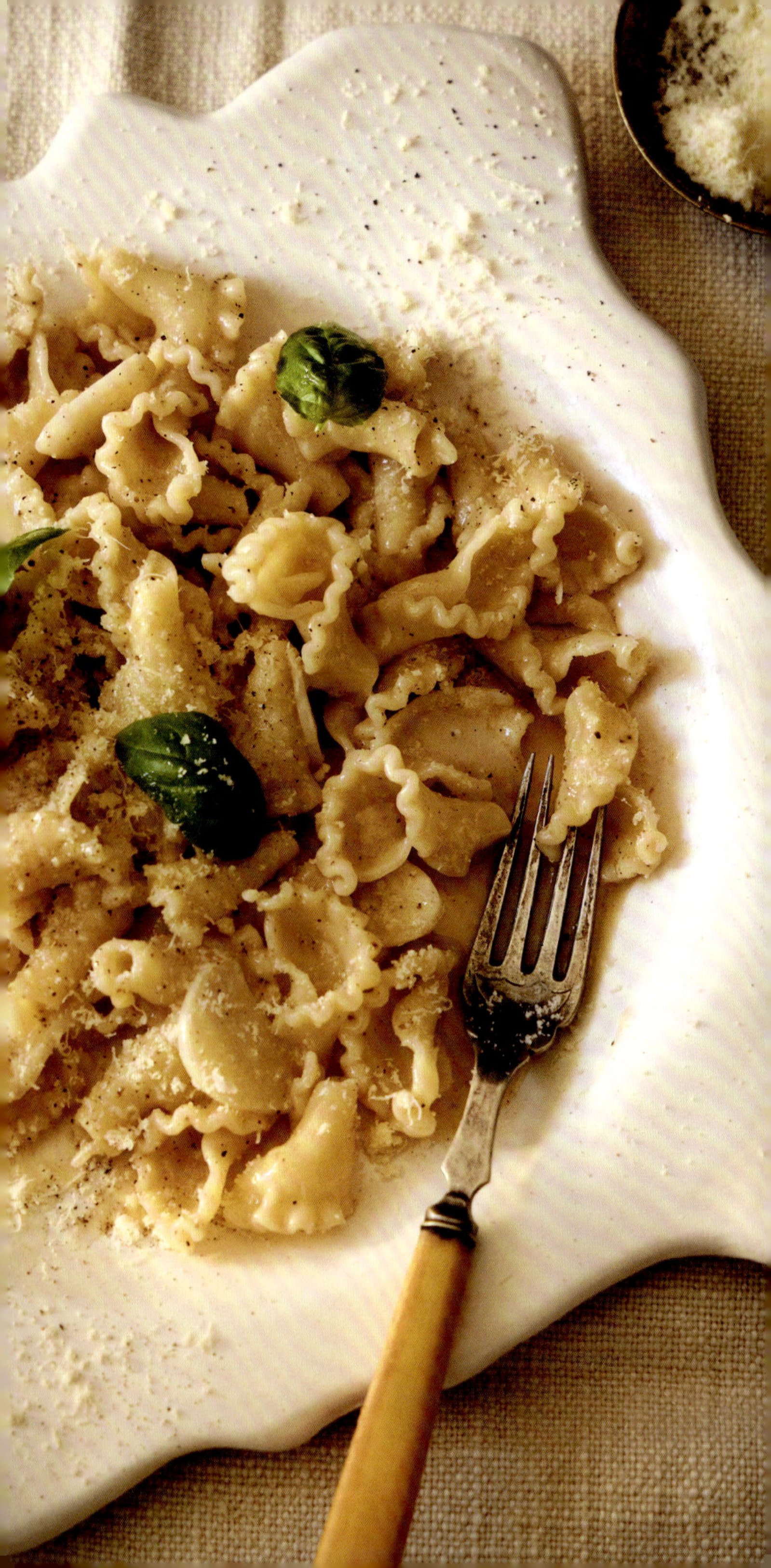

GROWN-UP BUTTERED PASTA

1 lb [455 g] mafalda corte, reginette, or other short pasta

10 Tbsp [145 g] cold salted butter, cubed

1 Tbsp olive oil

10 garlic cloves, thinly sliced

8 anchovy fillets

1 cup [240 ml] white wine

Kosher salt and freshly ground black pepper

Finely grated Parmesan, for serving

Basil, for garnishing (optional)

SERVES 4

I don't know a single child who doesn't love a bowl of warm, buttered pasta—a dish that's simple, satisfying, recognizable, safe, and comforting. This is my grown-up version, full of lusty garlic and anchovies in a butter sauce built on a white wine reduction. It's the dinner I make when there's "nothing to eat" in the house or when I just need my dinner to feel like a hug. For the best buttery sauce, be sure to add your butter and hot pasta cooking water bit by bit to help form the emulsion, like the process used when making beurre blanc (page 83).

[INSTRUCTIONS]

1   Bring a large pot of salted water to a boil and cook the pasta to al dente according to the package instructions. Drain the pasta, reserving 2 cups [475 ml] of the pasta cooking water.

2. While the pasta is cooking, in a large, deep skillet over medium heat, melt 2 Tbsp of the butter with the olive oil. Add the garlic and anchovies and cook for 4 to 5 minutes, stirring occasionally, until the anchovies are mostly melted and the garlic is beginning to lightly brown. Pour in the wine, increase the heat to medium-high, and scrape up any browned bits on the bottom of the skillet into the wine. Continue to cook until the wine is reduced by half, about 2 minutes. Reduce the heat to low, add a few cubes of the butter, and stir until a smooth sauce begins to form.

3. Add the cooked pasta to the garlic butter sauce along with ½ cup [120 ml] of the pasta cooking water and a few more cubes of butter. Stir until the butter is melted, then stir in more butter and more pasta cooking water, adding both in small doses until all the butter has been added and your pasta is coated with a smooth and rich sauce. (I just add splashes of the pasta water, but if you want to measure, use ¼ cup [60 ml] at a time.) You may not use all the pasta cooking water, but you'll need at least 1½ cups [180 ml] to achieve your glossiest sauce.

4. Season with salt and pepper. Divide the pasta among bowls and serve with Parmesan sprinkled on top. Garnish with a few basil leaves (if you wish).

BUTTER ROAST CHICKEN

1 whole chicken

Kosher salt

1 batch compound butter (page 48), at room temperature

SERVES 4

Spatchcocking (also known as butterflying) is my go-to way to roast a chicken. It cooks more quickly and evenly with lots of extra-crispy skin. A generous rubdown with compound butter before roasting is the secret to infusing the chicken with flavor and moisture while it roasts. You can pick any of the savory compound butter flavors on pages 50–51—my favorite for roast chicken is the Smoky Garlic Butter. Once the chicken is roasted and carved, slather it with additional butter before serving. The butter will pool across the warm meat like a silky sauce—it's so good, you'll be tearing into the chicken with your hands.

[**INSTRUCTIONS**]

1 Place the chicken breast side down on a rimmed baking sheet and pat dry. Using sharp kitchen shears, cut along each side of the backbone to remove and discard it. Use a sharp knife to make a notch on the top of the breastbone, then flip the chicken over and spread it open. Press down firmly on the breastbone to flatten the chicken—you should feel it pop apart when you do this. Pat the chicken nice and dry, then season it with kosher salt on all sides.

2   Using your hands, spread half the compound butter all over the chicken, pushing some up under the skin as well. This might feel gross, but it's very much worth it, flavor-wise. Arrange the chicken breast side up with the wings tucked in and refrigerate it as long as you have time for, up to 24 hours. If you don't have time for this step, it'll be alright!

3   Preheat the oven to 425°F [220°C] about 30 minutes before you're ready to roast the chicken. Transfer the baking sheet with the buttered chicken to the oven and roast until an instant-read thermometer inserted into the thickest part of the breast reads 165°F [75°C], about 45 to 60 minutes. The skin should be nicely browned and crisped and the meat no longer pink, and the juices should run clear when you poke the chicken with a knife.

4   Let the chicken rest for 10 minutes on a cutting board before carving. Dot with the remaining compound butter and serve.

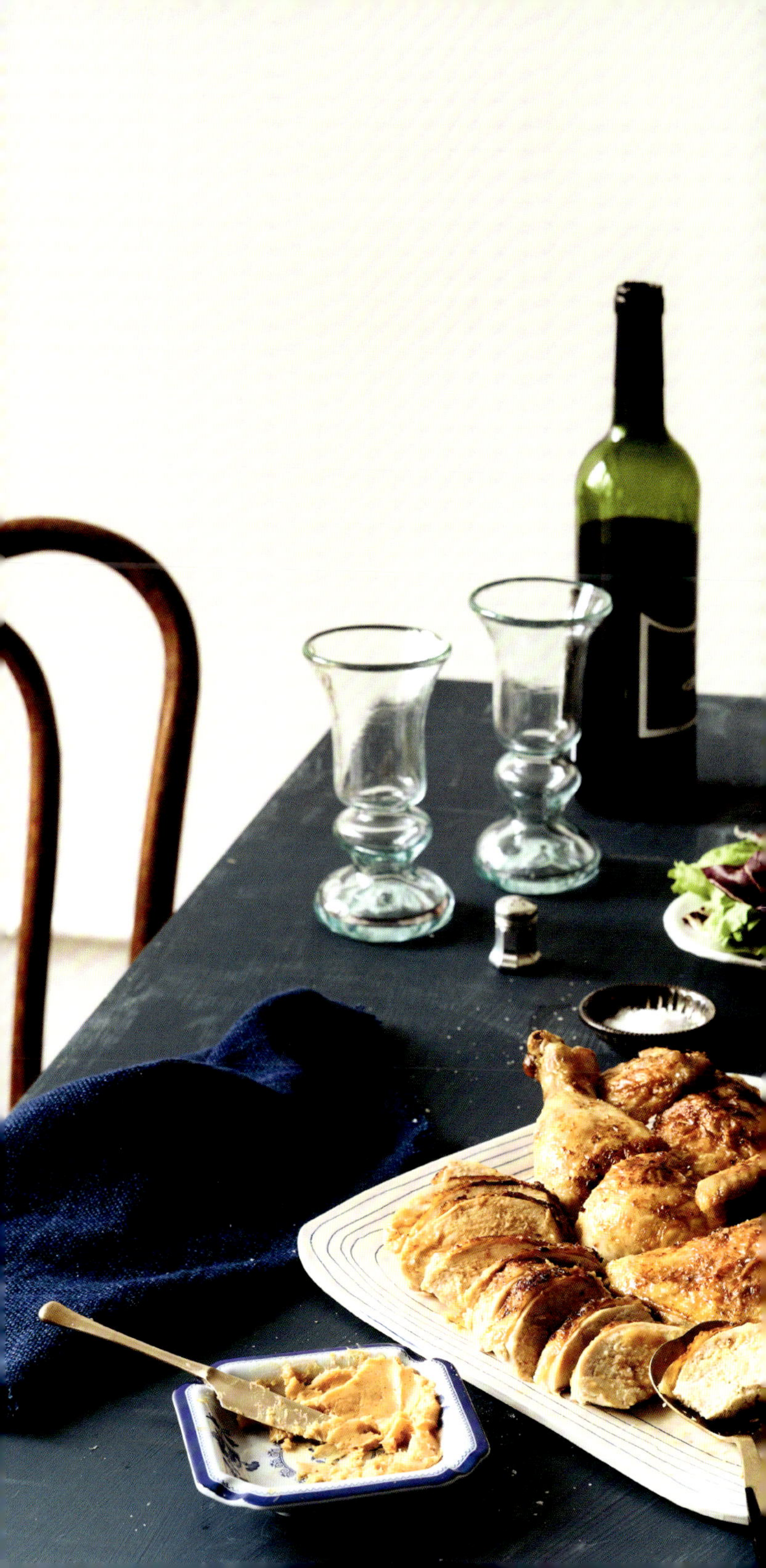

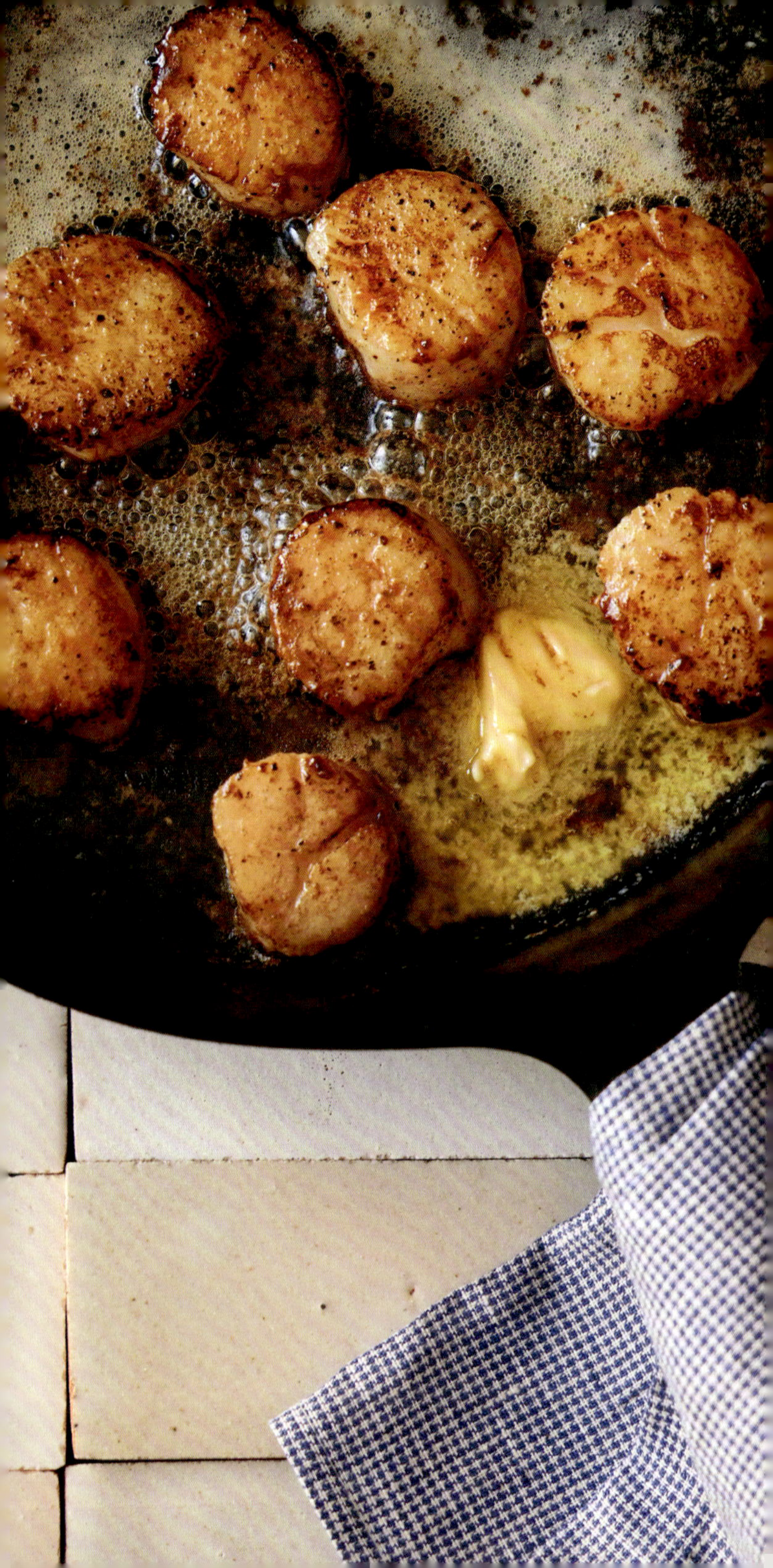

BUTTER-BASTED SCALLOPS WITH BEURRE BLANC

BEURRE BLANC

3 Tbsp dry white wine

1 Tbsp white wine vinegar

1 Tbsp finely chopped shallot

10 Tbsp [145 g] cold unsalted butter, cubed

Kosher salt and freshly ground black pepper

SCALLOPS

16 large fresh sea scallops (1¼ to 1½ lbs [½ to ¾ kg]), tendons removed

Kosher salt and freshly ground black pepper

2 Tbsp neutral oil, such as avocado oil

2 Tbsp cold unsalted butter, cubed

SERVES 4 Beurre blanc was the first sauce I learned to make in culinary school. The way a splash of white wine and handfuls of cold butter cubes transform into a thick, creamy, and silky warm sauce completely blew my mind. It feels like magic, but the chemistry is simple: The boiled-down white wine and vinegar base is highly acidic, so as you gradually whisk cold butter into it, the milk solids, which would normally separate from the fat, remain suspended in emulsion, creating a rich-bodied sauce. This classic butter sauce pairs with any simply cooked seafood or veg, but I like it best with scallops, which I pan sear and butter baste for the most even cooking and deepest caramelized crust.

[TO MAKE THE BEURRE BLANC]

1 In a small saucepan over medium-high heat, bring the wine, vinegar, and shallots to a boil. Lower to a simmer and continue to cook until the liquid is reduced by half and the steam no longer smells boozy, about 2 minutes.

2 Remove the pan from the heat and whisk in a few cubes of butter until just melted and a creamy emulsion forms. Return the pan to the lowest possible heat and continue adding butter, a few cubes at a time, whisking constantly. Add more butter after each addition is fully melted and emulsified. If the butter starts to melt too fast, remove from the heat to avoid breaking the sauce. Once the last bit of butter has been added, continue to whisk until the sauce is warmed all the way through, then remove from the heat and season with salt and pepper. Keep near the stove and whisk occasionally while you cook the scallops. Beurre blanc is best served as soon after making as possible. Do not try to rewarm it; this will break the sauce.

[**TO COOK THE SCALLOPS**]

3 Pat the scallops dry, then lightly season with salt and pepper.

4 In a large nonstick or cast-iron skillet over medium-high heat, warm the oil until it shimmers. Add the scallops and let them cook undisturbed until the bottoms are well browned, about 2 minutes. Add the butter and, once it has melted, flip the scallops. Gently tilt the pan and use a large spoon to pour the hot butter over the scallops. Continue cooking and basting until the scallops are firm and opaque, about 1 minute more. As each scallop is ready, transfer it to a plate—bigger scallops will take longer than smaller ones to finish cooking.

[**TO SERVE**]

5 Divide the sauce among 4 (ideally slightly warmed) plates, spreading it into a round puddle on each plate with the back of a spoon. Nestle 4 scallops on top of the sauce on each plate and serve. To turn this into a full meal, add some steamed asparagus or broccolini and serve with bread for mopping up all that good sauce. Beurre blanc does not keep, so enjoy it while it's fresh.

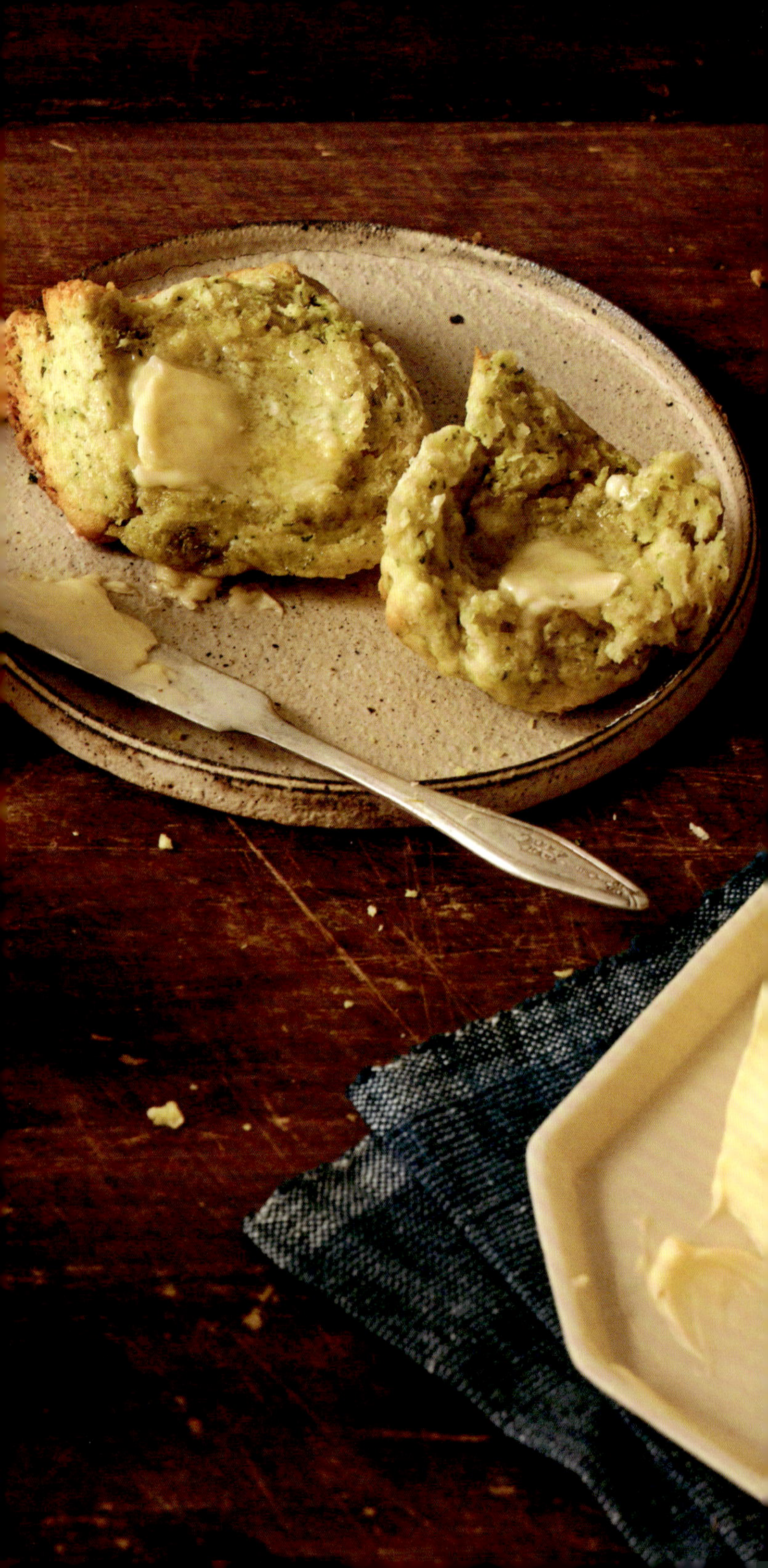

COMPOUND BUTTER BISCUITS

1 batch compound butter (page 48) or ½ cup [113 g] salted butter

1½ cups [180 g] all-purpose flour, plus more for surface

1 Tbsp granulated sugar

2 tsp baking powder

½ tsp kosher salt

½ cup [120 ml] buttermilk, plus more for brushing

MAKES 4 (RATHER LARGE) BISCUITS

A batch of any of the compound butter flavors on pages 50–51 will add fun new flavors to these buttermilk biscuits, but you can also make them with plain butter for a classic taste. Two other butter tricks are employed for this recipe: The first (which also works great for making pie crusts) is to chill the butter, grate it like cheese, and then just barely mix it into the flour. This removes the effort of rubbing butter into flour with your hands. More importantly, it ensures the dough is filled with many little pockets of cold butter, which will release leavening steam as they melt in the oven, helping to keep the biscuits fluffy and flaky. Pull-apart flakiness is also encouraged by the technique of folding and rolling out the dough repeatedly to create layers of butter, borrowed from the process of laminating butter into dough used in making croissants.

[INSTRUCTIONS]

1. If your compound butter is freshly made and soft, place it in the freezer to chill for at least 1 hour. If the butter has already been refrigerated, chill it in the freezer for at least 15 minutes.

2. Preheat the oven to 350°F [180°C]. In a mixing bowl, whisk together the flour, sugar, baking powder, and salt. Grate the chilled compound butter on the large holes of a box grater into the bowl. Use your hands to gently toss the grated butter until all the shreds are coated with flour. Pour half the buttermilk over the mixture and stir with a spoon to start to combine, then pour the rest of the buttermilk over and stir again until you have a shaggy, clumpy kind of dough. (The dough won't be cohesive at this point.)

3. Turn the dough out onto a lightly floured work surface and use a bench scraper (or a large metal spatula) and your hands to pat and press the dough into a square. Use the bench scraper or spatula to fold the dough in half over itself then pat it down into a square. Continue this folding and patting process five more times, adding flour as needed to keep the dough from sticking to the surface or your hands, until you have a square that's about 1½ in [4 cm] tall and 4 in [10 cm] across. Use your bench scraper or spatula to cut it into four even squares, then transfer to a parchment-lined baking sheet. At this point, you can chill the biscuits in the fridge until you're ready to bake them, for up to 24 hours. Before baking, chill in the freezer for 15 minutes to increase the rise and flakiness of the biscuits.

4 Brush the tops of the biscuits with buttermilk and then bake, rotating the baking sheet once halfway through, until the biscuits are golden brown, 25 to 30 minutes. Transfer to a cooling rack and serve while still warm, with butter.

> **NOTE** This recipe is easily doubled to make eight biscuits—you'll just have to make a double batch of compound butter for it.

> **TO MAKE THE BISCUITS GLUTEN-FREE** Substitute the all-purpose flour with an equal amount (1½ cups [180 g]) of an all-purpose gluten-free flour blend containing xanthan gum, and add an additional ½ tsp baking powder to the recipe.

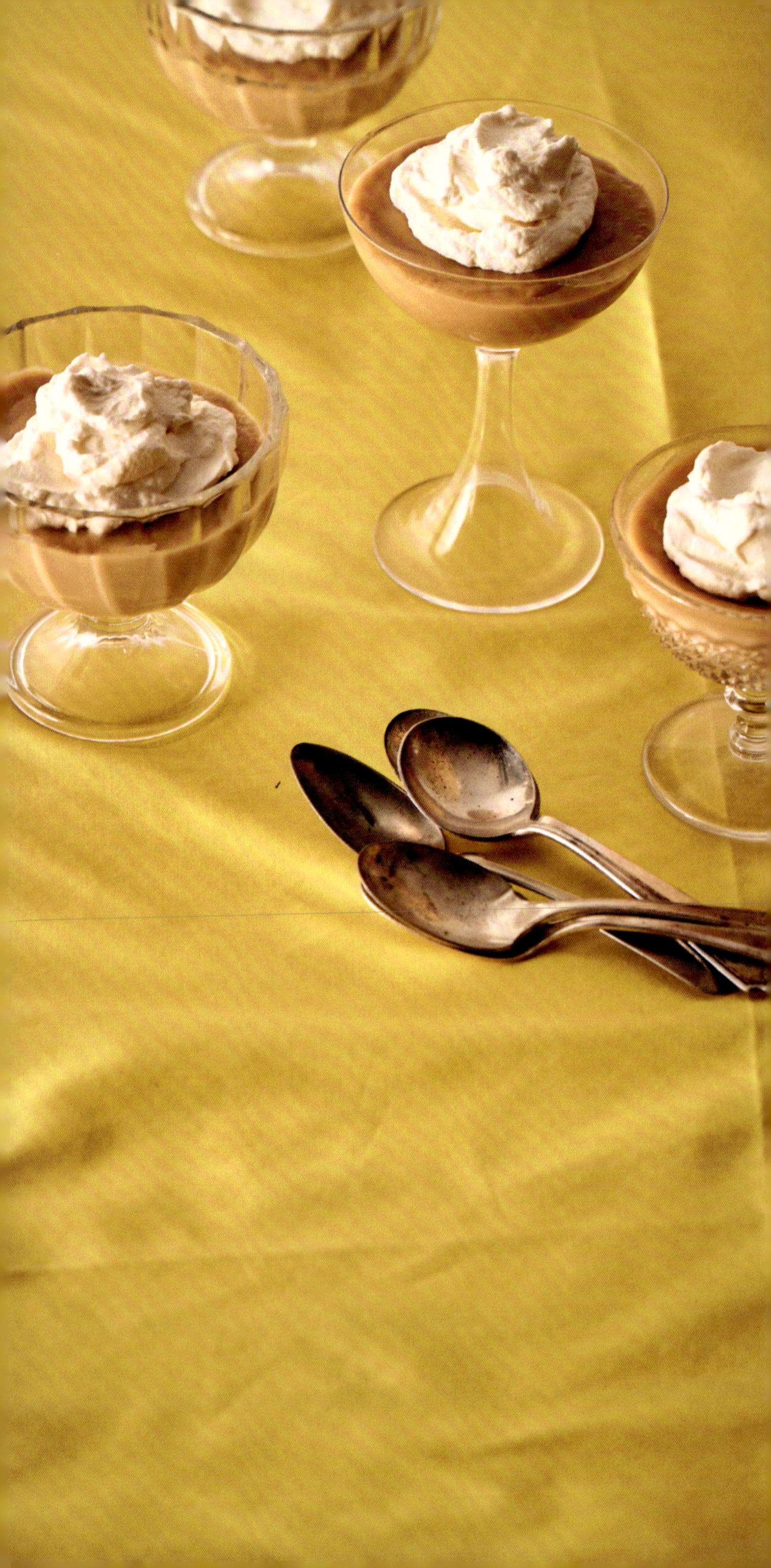

BUTTERSCOTCH PUDDING

½ cup [105 g] light brown sugar

4 Tbsp [56 g] unsalted butter

2 cups [475 ml] whole milk

3 egg yolks

3 Tbsp cornstarch

½ tsp kosher salt

1 cup [240 ml] heavy cream

1 tsp bourbon (optional)

Whipped cream, for serving (optional)

SERVES 4 TO 6

Butterscotch is essentially just melted butter and brown sugar cooked into a thick sauce or hardened into candies. Some might even call it "cheater's caramel." No one knows exactly why "scotch" is in its name, but some speculate it comes from "scorch," as in, scorch the sugar with the butter to form the flavor base of this pudding. There's no Scotch whisky in butterscotch, but you're welcome to add a dash if it strikes your fancy—personally, I find the warm, round flavor of bourbon better complements this decadent pudding. I use just enough cornstarch and egg yolks to set my butterscotch pudding while still letting a spoon glide silkily through each wonderfully wobbly spoonful. Finished by melting an extra pat of butter into the pudding before setting it, this is a dessert that pleases the inner child in all of us (as well as actual children—just skip the booze for them) and gracefully straddles the line between homey nostalgia and elegant excess.

[**INSTRUCTIONS**]

1. In a medium saucepan over medium-high heat, swirl together the sugar and 2 Tbsp of water until the mixture begins to bubble. Add 3 Tbsp of the butter and cook, swirling the pan occasionally, until the butter melts. Continue cooking until big, lazy bubbles are consistently appearing and the mixture thickly coats the back of a spoon, about 4 minutes.

2. Meanwhile, in a measuring cup or spouted bowl, whisk together the milk, egg yolks, cornstarch, and salt, whisking vigorously until smooth.

3. Reduce the heat to low and pour the heavy cream into the pan of caramel and cook, whisking constantly, until the caramel is fully dissolved into the cream, about 2 minutes. It will seize up dramatically at first, but just keep stirring!

4. Slowly pour the milk and egg mixture into the pot of caramel cream while whisking constantly. Raise the heat to medium and bring the pudding to a gentle boil, then cook, stirring with a spoon, for 2 minutes as the pudding continues to thicken. You'll know it's done when it thickly coats your spoon and a clear track is visible when you swipe your finger down the back of the spoon.

5. Remove the pudding from the heat and stir in the remaining 1 Tbsp of butter and the bourbon (if using). Divide the pudding among four 8 oz [240 ml] dessert cups or six 6 oz [180 ml] dessert cups and let cool completely. Once cool, cover with plastic wrap and chill to set for at least 3 hours before serving, topped with whipped cream, if desired. The pudding will keep in the fridge for up to 2 days.

CULTURED BUTTER OAT SHORTBREAD

1 cup [130 g] rolled oats

10 Tbsp [145 g] cultured, unsalted butter, at room temperature, plus more for the pan

⅓ cup [65 g] granulated sugar, plus more for topping

¾ cup [90 g] all-purpose flour

½ tsp kosher salt

MAKES ONE 8-INCH [20 CM] SHORTBREAD

The "short" of shortbread cookies refers not to height but to texture, as in tender and crumbly. This melt-in-your-mouth experience is thanks to the high butterfat content in the dough, which coats the flour and inhibits gluten formation by keeping the gluten strands short instead of long.

With so few ingredients, the flavor of butter really shines through in shortbread. Now is the moment to bake with the expensive butter—the slight tang and pleasant funk of cultured butter adds complexity to shortbread. Also adding intrigue here are ground oats, in a nod to an ingredient commonly used in Scottish-style shortbread. I grind my own oats instead of using oat flour because it gives the shortbread a more toothsome and nubbly texture that I prefer. If you don't have a food processor or blender, use an equal weight of store-bought oat flour.

[**INSTRUCTIONS**]

1 Preheat the oven to 325°F [165°C] and butter an 8 in [20 cm] fluted tart pan with a removable bottom (a springform pan will also work here, though it's not as cute).

2 In a food processor or a blender, pulse the oats until they're the consistency of a grainy flour, then set aside.

3 In a stand mixer fitted with the paddle attachment, beat the butter and sugar on medium speed until smooth. Add the ground oats, flour, and salt and beat on low just until the dough comes together. Tip the dough out into the prepared tart pan and press into an even layer with your hands. Poke the dough randomly across the surface with a fork, sprinkle the top with a bit of sugar, then let chill in the fridge for 20 to 30 minutes.

4 Place the pan on a rimmed baking sheet and bake for 35 to 40 minutes, rotating once halfway through, until the edges are golden brown. It will still be a bit soft in the center, but don't worry. It will set and crisp as it cools.

5 Let the shortbread cool for 15 to 20 minutes in the pan before removing the ring. Slice it into 8 (or 16) wedges while the shortbread is still warm, which prevents it from cracking and shattering. Let the shortbread cool completely before serving or storing in an airtight container for up to 1 week.

> **TO MAKE THE SHORTBREAD GLUTEN-FREE** Substitute the all-purpose flour with an equal amount (¾ cup [90g]) of an all-purpose gluten-free flour blend containing xanthan gum.

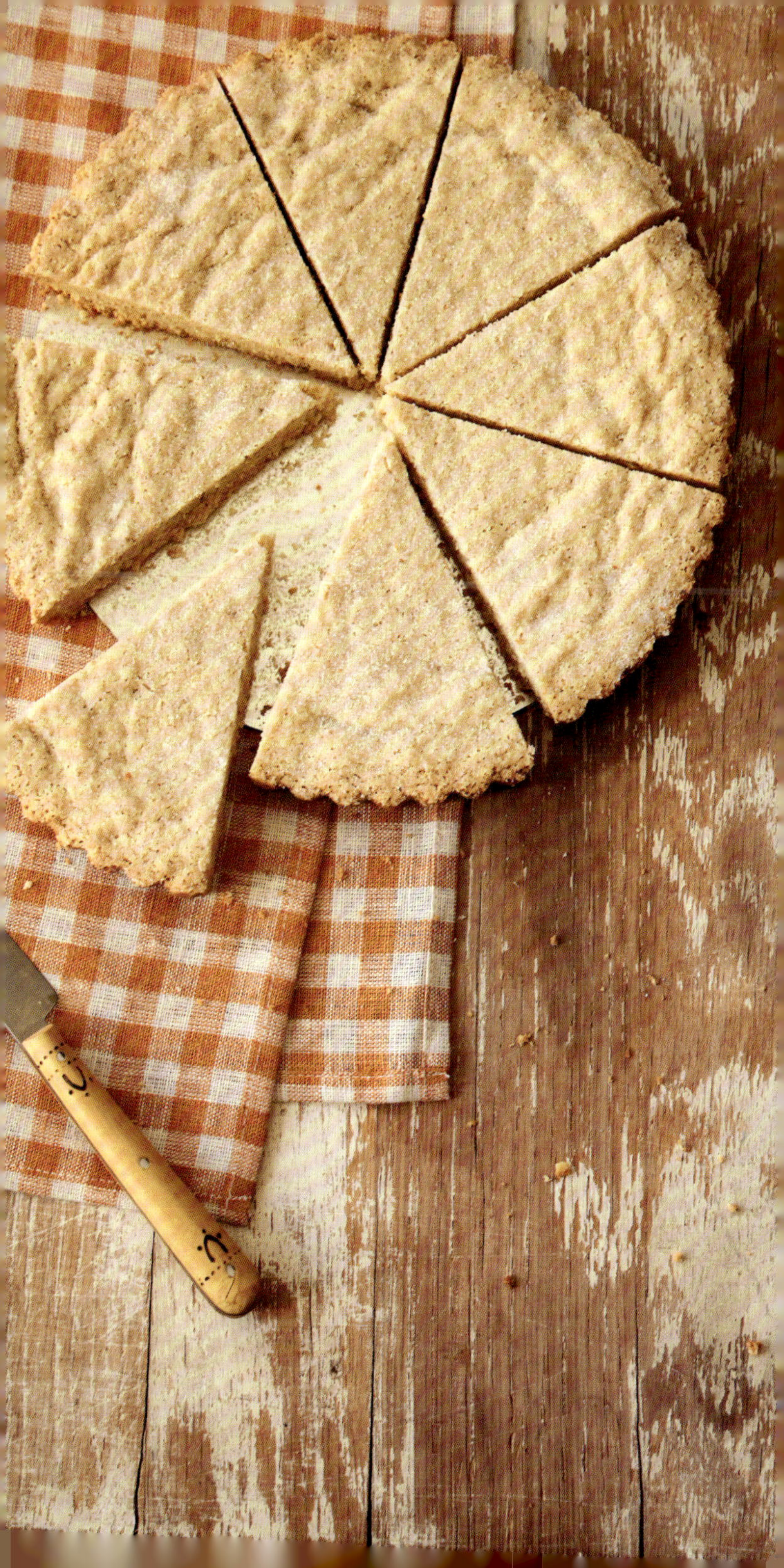

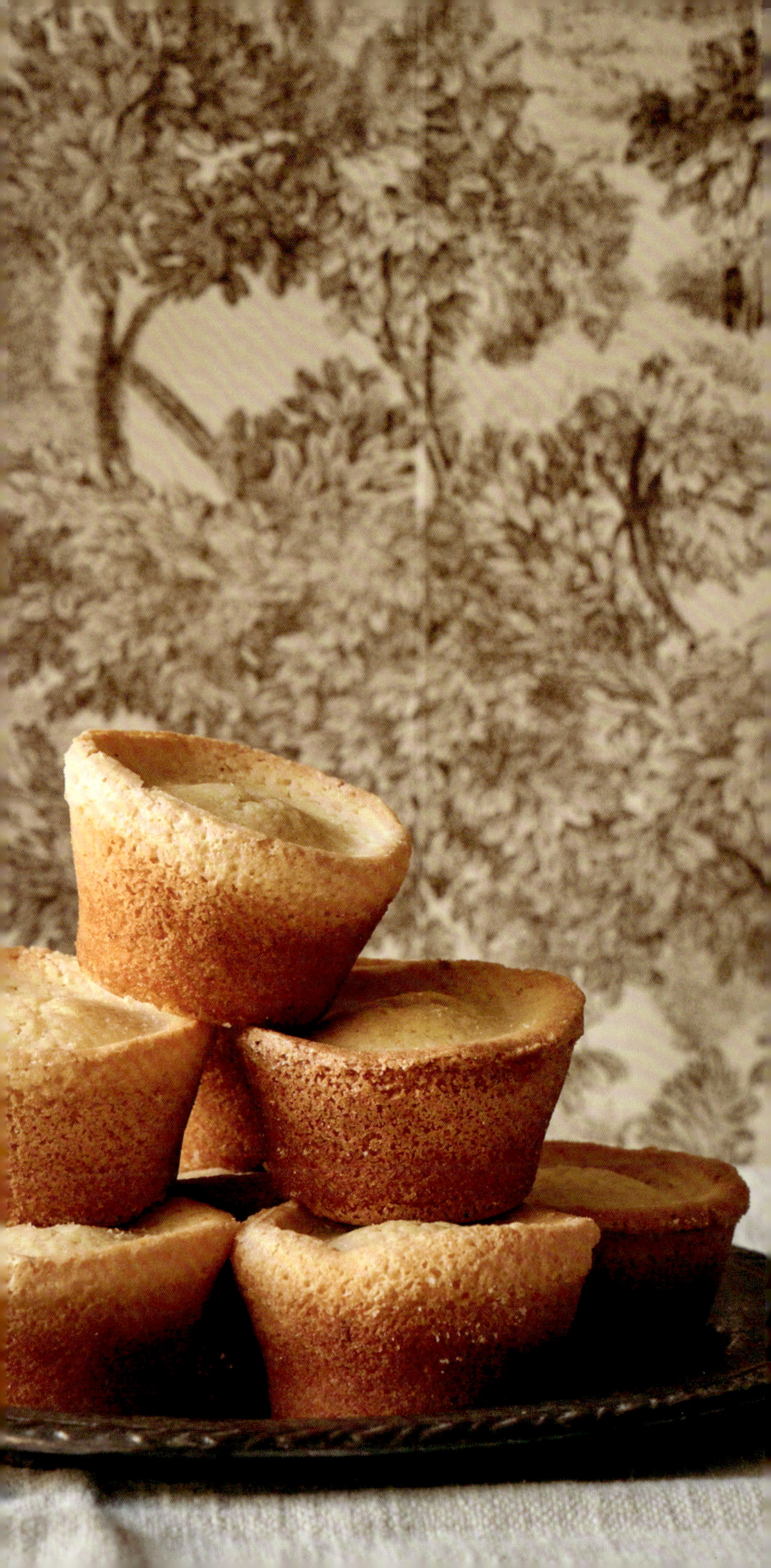

BROWN BUTTER MOCHI CUPCAKES

6 Tbsp [85 g] unsalted butter, plus more for the pan

1¼ cups [250 g] granulated sugar, plus more for the pan

1½ cups [360 ml] full-fat coconut milk, well stirred

2 large eggs

1 tsp vanilla extract

2 cups [325 g] mochiko flour (also known as sweet white rice flour or glutinous rice flour)

1 tsp baking powder

1 tsp kosher salt

MAKES 12 CUPCAKES

The bouncy-gooey texture of Hawaiian butter mochi cake is completely irresistible, but the contrast between the crispy caramelized crust and the chewy buttery center is my favorite thing about it. To get more of that textural contrast, I bake it as cupcakes instead of a cake. And to get even more caramel flavor, I brown the butter before using it in the batter. Browning butter is a classic technique in which you keep cooking the butter after it has melted until its naturally occurring sugars caramelize, changing the color to brown and the flavor to a richer, nuttier, and sweeter taste. It is magic in most baked goods, but especially in butter mochi.

[**INSTRUCTIONS**]

1. Preheat the oven to 350°F [180°C] and grease a muffin pan with butter. Sprinkle sugar into each mold, then rotate the pan over the sink until the sides of each mold are coated. Tap the pan vigorously over the sink to discard the excess sugar, then set aside.

2. In a medium saucepan over medium-high heat, warm the butter until melted and foaming, swirling often. Continue to cook, swirling, until the foam subsides and the butter turns golden brown (with flecks of dark brown in it) and smells nutty and caramelly, about 4 minutes. Remove from the heat, stir in the coconut milk, then transfer to a mixing bowl.

3. Whisk the sugar into the warm butter mixture and beat until combined, then whisk in the eggs and vanilla. Add the flour, baking powder, and salt and whisk until smooth. Divide the batter among the molds, filling each to just under the brim. Bake until the edges are golden brown and the tops bounce back when pressed, 40 to 45 minutes.

4. Let cool in the pan for 20 minutes, then lightly run a butter knife around the sides of each mold to release the mochi. Transfer to a wire rack to cool completely. Store in an airtight container at room temperature for up to 4 days... if you don't eat them all well before then.

NEW CLASSIC CHOCOLATE CHIP COOKIES

1 cup [226 g] unsalted butter

¾ cup [150 g] light brown sugar

½ cup [100 g] granulated sugar

2 large eggs, lightly beaten

1 tsp vanilla extract

1½ cups [180 g] all-purpose flour

1 cup [100 g] almond flour

1 tsp baking soda

1 tsp kosher salt

6 oz [170 g] milk chocolate chips

4 oz [115 g] bittersweet chocolate, coarsely chopped

MAKES ABOUT 36 COOKIES For my own (much tinkered with, perfect in my eyes) take on drop cookies, I made a few changes to the classic recipe. Most drop cookies are made by creaming together butter and sugar, which creates a fluffy, cakey texture. I prefer a denser, chewier cookie, so I make mine with melted butter. When you stir melted butter into sugar rather than beating air into unmelted butter, your cookies will naturally be less airy. And if you're going to melt butter, you might as well brown it for a richer, warmer, nuttier flavor. To increase the chewiness and the nuttiness, I also add some almond flour to my recipe. I make my cookies with a mix of milk chocolate chips

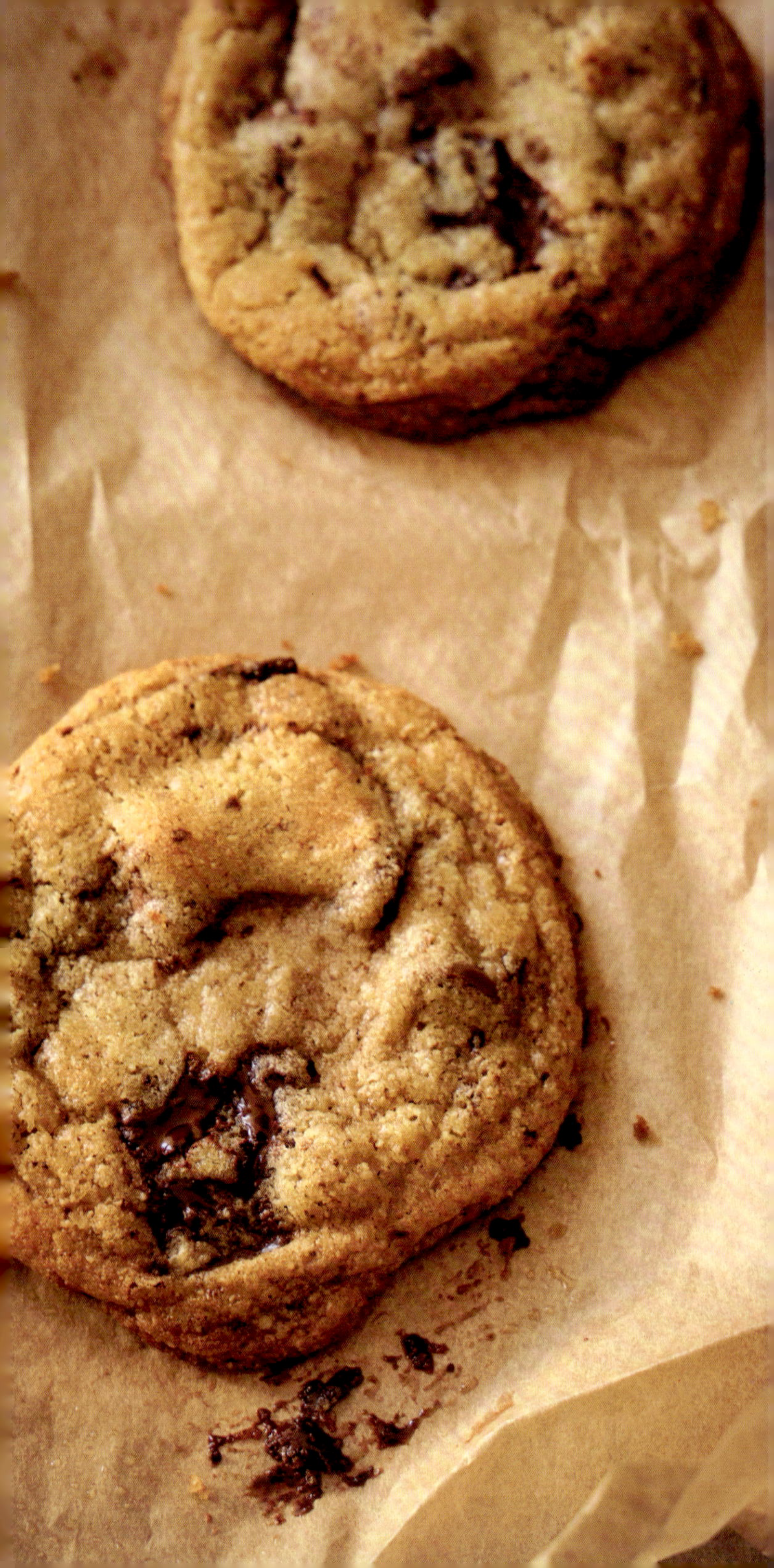

and chopped bittersweet chocolate for the best of both worlds—I like the way the chopped chocolate melts into the cookies, but you also get the classic chip texture.

[**INSTRUCTIONS**]

1 In a medium saucepan over medium-high heat, warm the butter until melted and foaming, swirling often. Continue to cook, swirling, until the foam subsides and the butter turns golden brown (with flecks of dark brown in it) and smells nutty and caramelly, about 4 minutes. Transfer to the bowl of a stand mixer and let sit for a few minutes, until cool enough to touch.

2 Add the brown sugar and granulated sugar to the butter in the stand mixer and beat on medium speed until well combined. Add the eggs and vanilla and beat until combined.

3 In a separate bowl, whisk together the flour, almond flour, baking soda, and salt, then gently tip into the butter mixture and beat on the lowest possible setting until a cohesive dough forms, stopping once halfway through to scrape down the sides of the bowl with a rubber spatula. Remove the bowl from the stand mixer and use a rubber spatula to fold in the chocolate chips and chopped chocolate. Cover and refrigerate for at least 8 hours (and no longer than 2 days). This chilled rest is essential for hydrating the dough, firming the butter, and ensuring a delightfully soft on the inside and crispy on the outside cookie texture.

4 Preheat the oven to 350°F [180°C] at least 20 minutes before baking. Line two baking sheets with parchment paper.

5 Scoop out about 2 Tbsp of the chilled dough, roll it into a ball, and place on a baking sheet. Repeat the process, arranging the dough balls about 2 in [5 cm] apart, until both sheets are full. Bake, rotating the sheets halfway through, until the cookies are just golden brown, about 10 minutes. They will appear slightly gooey in the center, but trust me, they're done! They'll firm up as they cool. Be careful not to overbake them or your soft center will be gone.

6 Let the cookies cool on the baking sheets for at least 10 minutes. Transfer them to a platter and eat them while they're still warm. Or move them to cooling racks to cool completely before storing. The cookies will keep in an airtight container for up to 5 days.

TO HAVE READY-TO-BAKE COOKIE DOUGH AT YOUR DISPOSAL Form the dough into balls on a parchment-lined baking sheet and freeze. Once frozen, transfer the dough to an airtight container or freezer bag and store in the freezer for up to 3 months. Bake directly from frozen following the instructions above, adding 2 to 4 minutes to the total bake time.

TO MAKE THE COOKIES GLUTEN-FREE Reduce the butter to ¾ cup [170 g] and substitute the all-purpose flour with an equal amount (1½ cups [180 g]) of an all-purpose gluten-free flour blend containing xanthan gum.

BIRTHDAY BUTTER CAKE

CAKE

1 cup [226 g] unsalted butter, at room temperature, plus more for the pans

1¼ cups [250 g] granulated sugar, plus more for the pans

2 cups plus 2 Tbsp all-purpose flour [255 g]

1 Tbsp baking powder

1 tsp kosher salt

1 cup [240 ml] buttermilk

1 tsp vanilla extract

4 large eggs, at room temperature

FROSTING

1 cup [90 g] cocoa powder

3½ cups [390 g] confectioners' sugar

1 tsp kosher salt

½ cup [120 ml] boiling water

1 tsp vanilla extract

1 cup [226 g] unsalted butter, at room temperature

MAKES ONE 8 IN [20 CM] TWO-LAYER CAKE; SERVES 10 TO 12

Traditionally, making a butter cake always started with creaming together butter and sugar until light and fluffy, mixing in eggs and milk, then finishing with flour and leavener. In the

1980s, cake queen Rose Levy Beranbaum changed the game by reversing the order and beating the butter with all the dry ingredients first. This technique yields cake with a more stable structure and a wonderfully tender, buttery crumb. It is both satisfyingly dense enough to sink your teeth into and airy enough to sort of melt in your mouth. I prefer the reverse creaming method for all those reasons, but also (importantly!) because it's a lot harder to mess up a cake this way! Coating the flour in fat means the gluten can't connect and glue together in the batter, which means you don't have to worry about overbeating it and ending up with a toughie.

In my mind there's only one way to serve yellow butter cake: with a thick layer of chocolate buttercream. I keep mine simple, made with lots of butter, cocoa powder, confectioners' sugar, and just the right amount of salt to balance it all out.

[TO MAKE THE CAKE]

1 Preheat the oven to 350°F [180°C]. Generously butter two 8 in [20 cm] cake pans, then generously sprinkle sugar into each pan and rotate them over the sink until the sides are coated. Tap the pans vigorously over the sink to discard the excess sugar, then set aside.

2 In the bowl of a stand mixer fitted with the paddle attachment, stir together the flour, sugar, baking powder, and salt on the lowest setting just until combined. Add the butter and beat on low until the mixture begins to appear sandy with some larger clumps of butter still visible. With the motor running on low, slowly pour in the buttermilk until the mixture is fully moistened. Increase the speed to medium and beat for 3 minutes. The batter should increase in volume and lighten in color during this time.

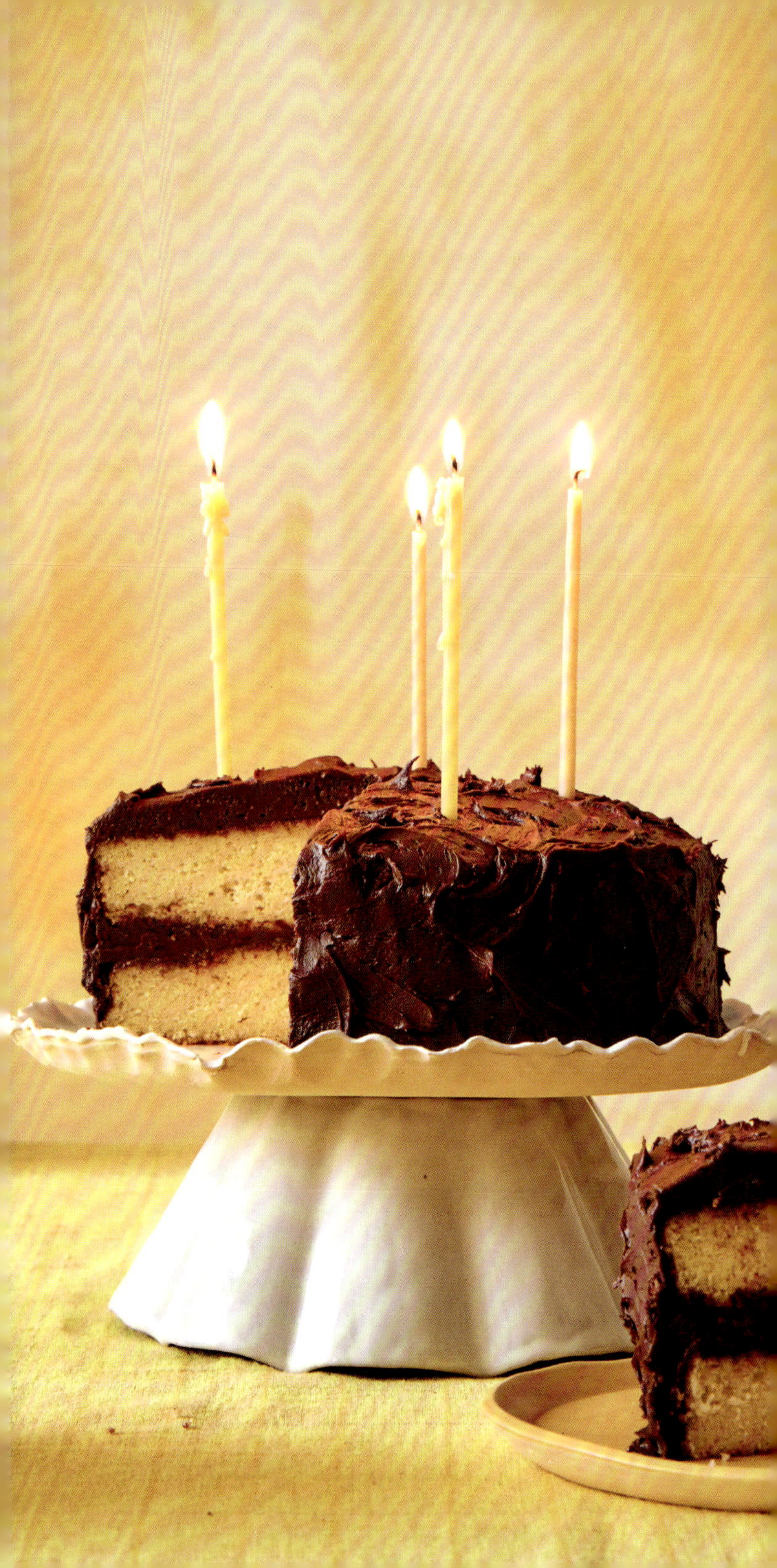

3 Add the vanilla and then add the eggs one at a time, beating until the batter is smooth (about 30 seconds) and scraping down the sides of the bowl after each addition. Divide the batter between the prepared pans, smoothing the tops, and banging each filled pan on the counter a few times to dislodge any bubbles.

4 Bake for 35 to 40 minutes, rotating the pans halfway through, until the cake is golden brown, pulls away from the edges of the pan, and springs back easily when lightly pressed. Let cool for 15 minutes in the pans before inverting the cakes onto a cooling rack. Let cool completely before frosting.

[TO MAKE THE FROSTING]

5 Sift the cocoa powder into the bowl of a stand mixer. Add 1 cup [120 g] of the confectioners' sugar and the salt and whisk by hand until fully combined. Pour in the boiling water and vanilla and stir with a rubber spatula until no clumps are visible. Affix the bowl to your stand mixer (use the paddle attachment) and add the remaining confectioners' sugar and the butter. Beat on low until the sugar is fully incorporated, then increase to high speed and beat until the frosting is smooth and glossy.

[TO ASSEMBLE THE CAKE]

6 Place a dollop of the frosting in the center of a cake plate to help secure the cake, then drape pieces of parchment or waxed paper around the outer edges of the plate to keep your plate clean. Place your first cake layer on top. Scoop about a third of the frosting on top of your first layer and gently spread it evenly across the top (you want your frosting layer to be about ¼ in [6 mm] thick).

Place the second cake layer on top of the frosting, gently press it down to secure it, then scoop the rest of the frosting on top and start working it down and around the edges of the cake until the whole cake is evenly coated. Use the back of a spoon to make swoops and swirls, or a long offset spatula to make a smooth, flat surface, as you wish. Once you're done frosting the cake, wiggle out the parchment or waxed paper and reveal your clean cake plate! (Give the papers to any drooling bystanders to lick.) If possible, chill the cake in the fridge for 1 hour before serving—it'll slice more easily if the frosting gets a chance to set. Store the cake, covered, at room temperature or in the fridge for up to 3 days. If refrigerated, bring to room temperature before serving.

TO MAKE THE CAKE GLUTEN-FREE Replace the flour with 2 cups plus 1 Tbsp [265 g] of an all-purpose gluten-free flour blend containing xanthan gum.

ACKNOWLEDGMENTS

Working on this book sweetened a dark and snowy winter with many buttery baked goods that warmed my heart and home. Thank you to my husband, **JACK**, for your love and support through the process, and for sampling every batch of shortbread. The mochi cupcakes will always be for you.

Thank you to my agent, **ADRIANA STIMOLA**, for making this project happen for me, and for being my tireless cheerleader. And to the team at Chronicle, thank you for trusting me to bring your idea of a little butter book to life. Thank you especially to my editor **CLAIRE GILHULY** for making the process so easy and for your careful and thoughtful edits.

LIZZIE VAUGHAN, creative director extraordinaire, brought together a powerhouse team of ladies in the Hudson Valley to make the gorgeous images you see in this book and guided us gently away from our crazier impulses on set. She also designed the clever layout of this book! **KATE JORDAN** made lighting and photographing every stack of butter and cupcakes all by herself look like a relaxing walk in the park in her lovely studio. **RAINA KATTELSON** brought each shot to life with her unique props, supplying everything from the most perfect antique mussel mold to my apron. I loved working as food stylist on set with all three of you—thank you for making this book look so good and for being such a joy to collaborate with.

I dove into learning everything I could about butter for this book, but the woman who dove even deeper into butter before me is **ELAINE KHOSROVA**. Her book, *Butter: A Rich History*, taught me more than I knew I needed to know about butter, and I'm truly grateful for and impressed by her research and journalism. I highly recommend you pick up a copy if you want to nerd out on butter too!

Last but not least: Thanks to all the **BUTTER MAKERS** who came before. I'm so glad to be living in a world and a time with such good butter in it.

INDEX

A

accessories	[28-29]
alternative butter	[37-38]
anchovies	
Green Goddess Butter	[50]
Grown-Up Buttered Pasta	[77-78]
Puttanesca Butter	[50]

B

Beurre Blanc	[83-84]
Birthday Butter Cake	[103-107]
Biscuits, Compound Butter	[87-89]
Brown Butter Mochi Cupcakes	[97-98]
butter	
accessories	[28-29]
alternative	[37-38]
boards	[65-67]
buying	[33-38]
clarified	[38, 43, 45]
compound	[48-51]
cultured	[35]
curls	[29, 62]
European-style	[36-37]
freezing	[39]
goat's-milk	[38]
health and	[16-17]
history of	[13-17]
Irish	[37]
keeping fresh	[39]
making	[18-21]
margarine vs.	[16]

measuring	[7]
molds	[28, 60–62]
mountain	[54]
nondairy	[37–38]
organic vs. grass-fed vs. pasture-raised	[35–36]
popularity of	[10–11]
rancid	[39]
refrigerating	[39]
salted vs. unsalted	[34]
sculptures	[59–62]
serving ideas for	[54, 59–62]
softening	[55]
sweet cream	[34–35]
using	[40–42, 69]
water buffalo	[38]
whipped	[53–54]
Butterscotch Pudding	[91–92]
buying tips	[33–38]

C

Cake, Birthday Butter	[103–7]
Chicken, Butter Roast	[79–80]
Child, Julia	[10]
chocolate	
Birthday Butter Cake	[103–7]
New Classic Chocolate Chip Cookies	[99–102]
Cilantro-Lime Butter	[50]
clarified butter	[38, 43, 45]
compound butter	[48–51]
Compound Butter Biscuits	[87–89]
cookies	
Cultured Butter Oat Shortbread	[93–94]
New Classic Chocolate Chip Cookies	[99–102]
coquillor	[28]
cultured butter	[35]
Cultured Butter Oat Shortbread	[93–94]
Cupcakes, Brown Butter Mochi	[97–98]

D
Doiron, Justine [65]

E
European-style butter [36–37]

G
garlic
    Grown-Up Buttered Pasta [77–78]
    Smoky Garlic Butter [50]
ghee [14, 38, 45]
goat's-milk butter [38]
Golden Butter [51]
grass-fed butter [35–36]
Green Goddess Butter [50]
Grown-Up Buttered Pasta [77–78]

H
Hot Honey Butter [51]

I
Irish butter [37]

L
limes
    Cilantro-Lime Butter [50]

M
Maître d'Hôtel Butter [50]
margarine [16]
McFadden, Joshua [65]
measuring [7]
Miso-Orange Butter [51]
Mochi Cupcakes, Brown Butter [97–98]
molds [28, 60–62]

N
nondairy butter [37–38]

O

Oat Shortbread, Cultured Butter	[93–94]
oranges	
Miso-Orange Butter	[51]
organic butter	[35]

P

Pasta, Grown-Up Buttered	[77–78]
pasture-raised butter	[35–36]
potatoes	
Pommes Anna (à la Anna)	[73–75]
Pudding, Butterscotch	[91–92]
Pumpkin Spice Butter	[51]
Puttanesca Butter	[50]
Raspberry-Thyme Butter	[51]

S

salted butter	[34]
Scallops, Butter-Basted, with Beurre Blanc	[83–85]
Scappi, Bartolomeo	[59]
sculptures	[59–62]
Seaweed Butter	[50]
Shortbread, Cultured Butter Oat	[93–94]
sweet cream butter	[34–35]

U

unsalted butter	[34]

V

Vanilla Bean Butter	[51]

W

water buffalo butter	[38]
whipped butter	[53–54]